A PRESOCRATICS READER

Second Edition

A PRESOCRATICS READER

Selected Fragments and Testimonia

Second Edition

Edited, with Introduction, by
PATRICIA CURD

Translations by
RICHARD D. MCKIRAHAN
and
PATRICIA CURD

Hackett Publishing Company, Inc.
Indianapolis/Cambridge

14   13   12   11   1   2   3   4   5   6   7

For further information, please address
  Hackett Publishing Company, Inc.
  P.O. Box 44937
  Indianapolis, Indiana 46244-0937

  www.hackettpublishing.com

Cover design by Listenberger Design & Associates
Interior design by Dan Kirklin
Composition by William Hartman
Printed at Victor Graphics, Inc.

Library of Congress Cataloging-in-Publication Data
A Presocratics reader : selected fragments and testimonia / edited,
with introduction, by Patricia Curd ; translations by Richard D.
McKirahan. — 2nd ed.
        p. cm.
    Includes bibliographical references.
    ISBN 978-1-60384-305-8 (pbk.) — ISBN 978-1-60384-306-5 (cloth)
    1. Philosophy, Ancient—Sources. 2. Pre-Socratic philosophers.
I. Curd, Patricia, 1949–   II. McKirahan, Richard D.
B187.5.P75 2010
182—dc22   2010019297

CONTENTS

PREFACE

A Presocratics Reader began as a revised and expanded version of the first section of *Readings in Ancient Greek Philosophy* (Hackett, 1st edition 1995). For a number of reasons, this is an excellent time to prepare a new edition of the *Reader,* and most of the changes will be incorporated into the next edition of *Readings in Ancient Greek Philosophy.*

Since 1995 and 1996 when this volume was put together, Presocratic studies have grown rapidly. Exciting new material has been discovered: the Strasbourg Papyrus with its previously unknown lines of Empedocles, and the Derveni Papyrus, which shows how Presocratic philosophy was adopted into the wider intellectual world of ancient Greece. There have been new studies published, and numerous international conferences: scholars have asked novel questions, and offered fresh interpretations. In this new edition, I have revised all of the introductory material (in many cases to take advantage of recent interpretations), and have included much of the new material (especially on Empedocles) that has come to light. The fragments in the Heraclitus and Empedocles chapters have been reordered, and the chapter on the Sophists has been changed in order to provide longer selections and a view of the Sophists more in keeping with contemporary scholarship. Finally, this edition includes the text of the intriguing Derveni Papyrus.

For *A Presocratics Reader,* the most important development has been Richard D. McKirahan's complete revision of his excellent volume, *Philosophy Before Socrates,* for its second edition. The translations from this new edition of *Philosophy Before Socrates* form the backbone of *A Presocratics Reader,* and in revising this little book, I have had the advantage of working through the new material and corresponding with Professor McKirahan. Suggestions from those who have used *A Presocratics Reader* (including students and colleagues here at Purdue University) have been very helpful, and I have tried to incorporate as many of them as possible.

This collection is meant as a sourcebook of moderate length; it is not a complete collection of the fragments and testimonia for the figures included here. My aim has been to provide a good selection from the early Greek philosophers, along with some of the ancient reports about them, with minimal editorial intrusion. I have strong views about many issues in Presocratic philosophy, but I have refrained from imposing them on the reader. Those who want more scholarly intervention should consult the suggested readings at the end of each section. These readings (some introductory and some more advanced) will offer interpretations, arguments, and further references so that anyone beginning here can quickly enter the world of Presocratic scholarship.

In the last two years I have worked with Richard McKirahan as he was preparing the second edition of *Philosophy Before Socrates*. He allowed me to use a version of the new text in a seminar with upper-level undergraduates and graduate students at Purdue University, and we discussed many questions of translation and interpretation. As always, I have learned much from Richard, even—and perhaps mostly—when we disagree. (I am happy to note that over these years we have come to have more agreements.) I am grateful for his comments and suggestions on my work over the years, including this project. I have also benefited from the Pythagorean expertise of Professor Carl Huffman, to whom I extend thanks.

The editors at Hackett Publishing have supported *Readings in Ancient Greek Philosophy* and *A Presocratics Reader* from the beginning, and I am grateful to them, and especially to Brian Rak and Liz Wilson.

ON ABBREVIATIONS
AND NOTES

The standard text collection for the Presocratics is H. Diels and W. Kranz, *Die Fragmente der Vorsokratiker* (6th edition, Berlin, 1951, and later printings), commonly referred to as *DK*. This collection has defined the scholarly conventions for referring to Presocratic texts, whether in Greek, Latin, or a modern translation. For each Presocratic philosopher DK assigns an identifying number: for example, Heraclitus is 22 and Anaxagoras is 59. DK uses the letter *A* to indicate testimony from ancient sources about that person, and the letter *B* to refer to what are taken to be direct quotations from that figure's work. These quotations are also referred to as the *fragments*, since all we have are small sections from longer works. Furthermore, DK identifies the testimonia and fragments by unique numbers. Thus text identified as 22A2 refers to Heraclitus (22) testimony (A) number two (2); and text identified as 59B12 refers to Anaxagoras (59) fragment (B) number twelve (12).

In this volume, DK numbers (where available) accompany every quotation; when all the passages in a chapter come from the same section of DK, the particular Presocratic's identifying number (22 or 59 in the examples just given) is listed only for the first passage. Hence fragment 1 from Anaxagoras will be identified as "(59B1)" and fragment 12 as "(B12)." Where texts come from more than one section, complete identifying DK numbers will be used as appropriate. In all cases, the source of the testimony or fragment from which DK drew the text appears at the end of the passage. For those texts that are not included in DK, the standard textual identification for the source is given along with the indication "not in DK." Where proper names follow textual references, the reference is to the editor of the standard edition of the relevant text. For example, in the Heraclitus chapter, the entry "Proclus, *Commentary on Plato's Alcibiades I* 117, Westerink" following selection 8 (B104) indicates that the fragment comes from Proclus' *Commentary on Plato's Alcibiades I*, and can be found on p. 117 of L. G. Westerink's 1954 edition of the text. References to two major papyrus collections use the standard abbreviations "P.Herc." and "P.Oxy."[1]

Unless otherwise indicated, translations are by Richard D. McKirahan. In the few places where I have modified his translations, "tmpc" appears in the source identification line; where I have translated the entire passage, "tpc" appears. All of the translations in Chapter 9 (Anaxagoras) are mine.

Notes on the texts are scattered throughout this collection. Notes from the translator (McKirahan) are marked as such; all other notes are mine.

Finally, in the translations of quoted passages from ancient authors, I use a system of brackets:

(. . .) Parenthetical comment in the ancient text
<. . .> Supplements to the text (either proposed by scholars, or added by the translator for the sake of clarity)
[. . .] Alternative possible translations, explanatory remarks, or context for the quoted passage

1. P.Herc. is the Herculaneum Papyri, followed by the classification number of the papyrus. (More information can be found at http://163.1.169.40/cgi-bin/library?site=localhost&a=p&p=about&c=PHerc&ct+0&1=en&w=utf-8.) P.Oxy. is the Oxyrhynchus Papyri, followed by the classification number of the papyrus. (More information can be found at http://www.papyrology.ox.ac.uk/POxy/.)

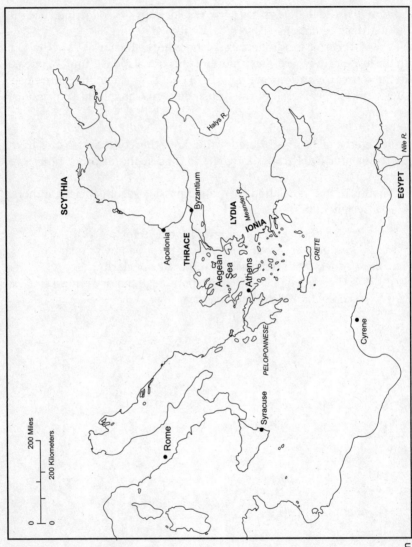

The Eastern
Mediterranean

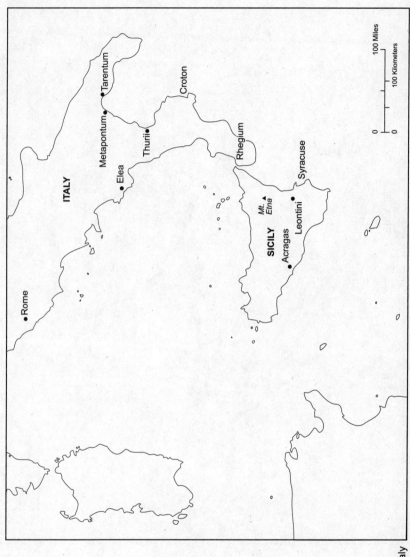

Sicily and
Southern Italy

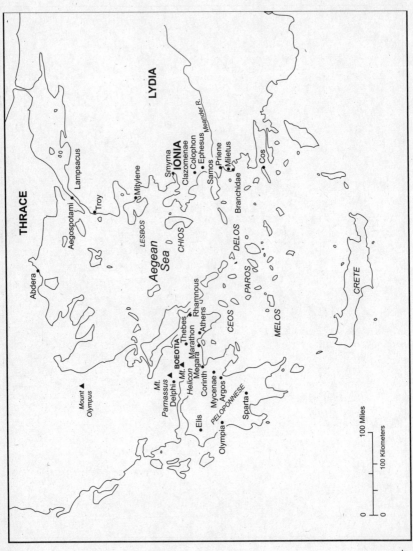

THRACE

LYDIA

IONIA

Lampsacus

Aegospotami

Troy

Abdera

LESBOS

Mitylene

Smyrna
Clazomenae
Colophon
Ephesus
Samos
Priene
Miletus
Branchidae
Cos

Meander R.

CHIOS

Aegean
Sea

DELOS

PAROS

CEOS

MELOS

CRETE

Mount
Olympus

Mt.
Parnassus
Delphi

Mt.
Helicon

Thebes
BOEOTIA
Marathon
Rhamnous
Megara
Athens
Corinth
Mycenae
Argos
PELOPONNESE
Sparta

Elis

Olympia

100 Miles

100 Kilometers

0

0

Greece and
Western Asia Minor

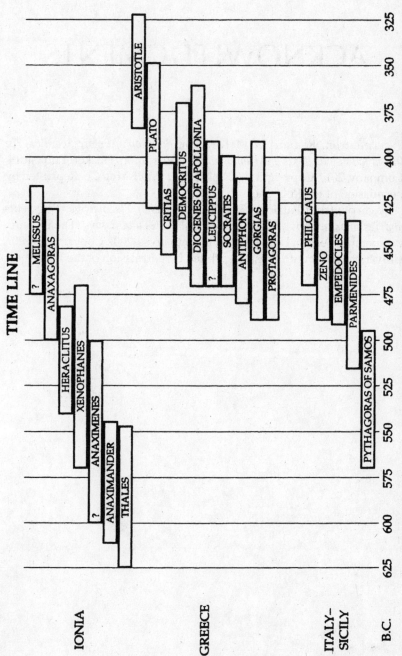

TIME LINE

IONIA

GREECE

ITALY–
SICILY

B.C.

Given the uncertainty of our evidence for the dates of the Presocratic philosophers, this time line is only approximate.

ACKNOWLEDGMENTS

Excerpts from Richard D. McKirahan, *Philosophy Before Socrates: An Introduction with Texts and Commentary,* 2nd edition, Hackett Publishing Company, 2010. Copyright © 2010, Hackett Publishing Co. Reprinted by permission of the Publisher.

Excerpts from Patricia Curd, *Anaxagoras of Clazomenae: Fragments and Testimonia. Texts and Translation with Notes and Essays* (The Phoenix Presocratics Series), University of Toronto Press, 2007. Copyright © 2007, University of Toronto Press. Reprinted by permission of the Publisher.

1. INTRODUCTION

Ancient tradition says that Thales of Miletus predicted an eclipse of the sun. Although we know none of the details of this supposed prediction, the event (an eclipse in 585 BCE) has traditionally marked the beginning of philosophy and science in Western thought. Aristotle, who was one of the earliest to think critically about the history of philosophy, speculated about why this kind of inquiry should have begun in Miletus, a Greek city on the Ionian coast of Asia minor (in what is now Turkey); like later scholars who have asked this question, Aristotle was unable to find an answer. So the circumstances surrounding the beginning of philosophy remain unclear; perhaps the question is unanswerable. Nevertheless, Thales, the titular first philosopher, stands at the beginning of a great tradition of rational inquiry and critical thought about the world and the place of human beings in it that continues to the present day.

Thales was the first of a succession of thinkers known as the Presocratics who lived in Greece in the sixth and fifth centuries BCE.[1] These thinkers do not belong to any unified school of thought, and they differed dramatically in their views. Yet they share intellectual attitudes and assumptions and they all display an enthusiasm for inquiry that justifies studying them as a group. It cannot be merely Thales' reported prediction of an eclipse that can justify our thinking of him as the first Western philosopher and scientist—after all, both the Babylonians and the Egyptians had complex astronomies. Nevertheless, for Aristotle and those who came after him, Thales, and his fellow-Milesians

---

1. The name "Presocratics" comes from 19th-century classical scholars, who saw a fundamental break between the interests and methods of our group of thinkers and Socrates (470–399 BCE), and who regarded Socrates' interests in ethics as a radical advance in Western thought. Few would now agree with that evaluation, and it is worth pointing out that several of our Presocratics were actually contemporaries of or younger than Socrates. So, as a descriptive label, the name "Presocratics" is misleading, but as a designator for a recognized group of thinkers, it is quite useful, and I shall use it here in that sense. For more on this issue, see articles in Long and in Laks and Louguet.

Anaximander and Anaximenes, shared an outlook that truly marks the
beginning of philosophical inquiry. Part of this was a willingness to
speculate and give reasons based on evidence and argument. Another
aspect was a commitment to the view that the natural world (the entire
universe) can be explained without needing to refer to anything beyond
nature itself. For instance, Thales seems to have thought that everything
is from water (although it is not clear whether he thought that water is
the origin of all things, or that everything really is water in some form
or another). This may strike us as a naïve and overly simplistic claim.
Yet Aristotle saw in Thales' views something that suggested that Thales
had reasons and arguments for them:

> [T]hey do not all agree about how many or what kinds of such prin-
> ciples there are, but Thales, the founder of this kind of philosophy,
> stated it to be water. (This is why he declared that the earth rests on
> water.) Perhaps he got this idea from seeing that the nourishment
> of all things is moist, and that even the hot itself comes to be from
> the moist and lives on it (the principle of all things is that from
> which they come to be)—getting this idea from this consideration
> and also because the seeds of all things have a moist nature; and
> water is the principle of the nature of moist things.
>   (Aristotle, *Metaphysics* 1.3 983b18–27 = DK 11A12)

From Aristotle's comments, it is clear that he thought that Thales' claim
was based on reasoning from observational evidence.

We may contrast Thales' account of the character of the natural world
with the story Hesiod tells (probably in the century before Thales) about
the origin of the cosmos:

> Tell me these things, Muses, who dwell on Olympus,
> From the beginning, and tell me, which of them was born first.
> First of all Chaos came into being. Next came
> broad-breasted Gaia [Earth], the secure dwelling place forever of all
> the immortals who hold the peak of snowy Olympus.
> And murky Tartaros [Underworld] in a recess of the broad-roaded
>   Earth,
> and Eros [Love], who is the most beautiful among the immortal
>   gods, who
> loosens the limbs and overpowers the intentions and sensible plans
> of all the gods and all humans too.

From Chaos there came into being Erebos [Darkness] and black
   Night.
From Night, Aithēr [bright upper air] and Hemera [Day] came into
   being,
which she conceived and bore after uniting in love with Erebos.
Gaia first brought forth starry Ouranos [Heaven]
equal to herself, to cover her all about
in order to be a secure dwelling place forever for the blessed gods.
She brought forth long mountains, beautiful shelters of divine
Nymphs who live in wooded mountains,
and also, without delightful love, gave birth to the barren sea,
Pontos, raging with its swelling waves. Then,
bedded by Ouranos, she gave birth to deep-swirling Ocean
and Koios and Kreios and Hyperion and Iapetos
and Theia and Rhea and Themis and Mnemosyne
and Phoebe with a golden wreath and lovely Tethys.
After them, last of all, was born crafty-minded Kronos,
the most terrible of the children, and he hated his mighty father.
                                        (Hesiod, *Theogony* 114–38)

Hesiod requests the help of the Muses for the claims he will make. He
then reports on the births of the gods with the Muses' authority as his
source. In relying on the Muses, Hesiod does not infer his account of
the cosmos from natural evidence. Nor does he think that appeals to
evidence are necessary: the divine warrant offered by the Muses is sufficient for his purposes. Hesiod's account of the origins of the universe
(his cosmogony) is in fact a story of the origins of the gods (a theogony).
Each aspect of the cosmos is identified with the distinct characteristics
and personality of a god, who controls that part of the universe. The
change from the state of chaos to the presence of Gaia (Earth), Tartaros
(the deepest underworld), Eros (desire), Erebos (the darkness under the
earth), and Night is not explained in this passage.[2] Earth, Tartaros, and
Eros simply came to be; there is no attempt to explain how this happened or justify why they came to be at exactly this moment rather
than another. Once Eros is present, the model of generation is primarily sexual, although we are told that Gaia (Earth) gave birth to Pontos
(sea) "without delightful love." These gods who, in some sense, *are* the

2. Hesiod says that Chaos "came into being"; there is no explanation for this
coming-to-be.

different parts of the universe, behave like humans in their desires, emotions, and purposes. As in the Egyptian, Sumerian, and Hebrew creation myths, the Hesiodic story makes no clear distinction between a personality and a part of the cosmos: The natural and the supernatural coincide. Since Hesiod feels no compunction about asserting his claims without reasons to support them, he seems to think that the proper response to the story is acceptance. The hearer or reader should not subject it to critical scrutiny followed by rational agreement or disagreement.

While the Presocratics rejected both the kind of account that Hesiod gave and his attitude toward uncritical belief, we must take care not to overstate the case: In the fragments of the Presocratics we shall find gaps in explanation, appeals to the Muses, apparent invocation of divine warrant, breaks in the connection between evidence and assertion. Despite all these apparent shortcomings, these early Greek thinkers took a bold leap in adopting a critical attitude. In the case of the Milesians, for instance, we find each proposing something different as the ultimate foundational reality of the cosmos. Anaximander, who followed Thales, apparently rejected the idea that water is the basic stuff; in its place he posited a single reality that he called the boundless (or the indefinite), something with no specific characteristics, out of which arise the other ingredients of the cosmos. Anaximander's follower Anaximenes, in turn rejects the boundless, apparently arguing that it was just too indefinite to do the job Anaximander required of it. Anaximenes claimed that air was the foundational stuff. Moreover, he seems to have seen that there was a gap in the earlier Milesian theories: Thales and Anaximander provided no mechanism to account for the transformations of their basic stuff. Anaximenes remedies this by proposing the processes of condensation and rarefaction: as air becomes more rarified or compacted, other stuffs are produced. Despite the disagreements among them, even this brief view shows that the Milesians worked within a shared framework of argument and justification.

Having adopted this critical attitude, the early Greek thinkers faced the question of what a human could justifiably claim to know. The Milesians might make claims about the basic stuff of the cosmos, and might give arguments for these claims, but how could they claim to have knowledge about an original or basic state of the universe, which they had never experienced? Hesiod would have an answer to this question: He could say that his information came from the Muses, and he could call on them to authenticate the truth of his claims about the coming-to-be of the gods. In the same way, we find Homer calling on the Muses when he wants to offer a catalogue of the leaders of the expedition to Troy. Because the Muses are divine they are immortal; since they were present for the gathering of the ships, they are appropriate as witnesses and can provide assurance that the story Homer tells is true:

> Tell me now Muses, who have dwellings in Olympus
> for you are goddesses and present and know everything,
> while we hear only rumor and we know nothing;
> Who were the Greek commanders and leaders?
> The throngs I could never tell nor name,
> Not even if ten tongues, ten mouths belonged to me,
> a voice unbroken, and a bronze heart within me,
> Unless the Olympian Muses, daughters of aegis-holding
> Zeus, put into my mind those who came below Ilion.
>
> (Homer, *Iliad* 2.484–92; tpc)

Although the contexts differ, Homer and Hesiod use the same invocation of the Muses to guarantee their claims: historical for Homer, religious and cosmogonical for Hesiod. Xenophanes of Colophon specifically rejects this justification. "By no means," he says (21B18), "did the gods intimate all things to mortals from the beginning, but in time, by inquiring, they discover better" (tpc). In rejecting divine authority for their claims, the Presocratics invite inquiry into the sources of human knowledge. A tantalizing mention of this problem appears in a fragment from Alcmaeon, who echoes Homer's claims that the gods know all things, but apparently offers a more pessimistic outlook for humans: "Concerning the unseen, the gods have clarity, but it is for men to conjecture from signs . . ." (DK24B1; tpc). We do not have the end of the fragment, but it is clear that Alcmaeon is contrasting the limited epistemic status of humans with the exalted certainty that the gods enjoy.

We find the Presocratics considering what separates sure and certain knowledge from opinion or belief, and the roles of sense perception and thought in acquiring knowledge, and, indeed, worrying about the very possibility of such knowledge. Moreover, as competing theories about the cosmos appear, the problem of theory justification comes to the fore. Sometimes, as with the three Milesians, justification might be a question of which theory appears to fit the evidence best; but there is another aspect to theory justification, and that is the metatheoretical question about what constitutes a genuine theory, regardless of the particular content. This problem is raised most strikingly by Parmenides of Elea, and his powerful arguments about what can be genuinely thought and said haunt the Greek thinkers who come after him, including Plato and Aristotle.

Although we call these early Greek thinkers "philosophers," they would probably not have called themselves by that name.[3] They were active in many fields, and would not have thought that astronomy, physics, practical engineering, mathematics, and what we call philosophy were separate disciplines, and most would not have thought that engaging in study of any of these areas would preclude them from being active in politics. In a society that was still more oral than literary, in which books (as scrolls, not codices) were just beginning to be written and distributed, the Presocratics thought and wrote about an astounding number of things. In the ancient testimonies about the Presocratics, we find reports of writings on physics, ethics, astronomy, epistemology, the gods and human worship of them, mathematics, metaphysics, meteorology, geometry, politics, the mechanism of sense perception, history (including the history of their own field), and even painting and travel. They wrote in poetry and they wrote in prose. They were as interested in the question of how a human being ought to live as in the question of the basic stuffs of the cosmos. Struggling to make philosophical notions clear in a language that did not yet have technical philosophical terms, they used elegant images and awkward analogies, straightforward arguments and intricate paradoxes. Much of their work has not survived, and we know of most of it only through the reports and quotations given by later philosophers and historians.[4] These later scholars preserved or referred to those parts of Presocratic thought that were most relevant for their own work; therefore most of what has come down to us are fragments of and testimonia about their views on natural philosophy, metaphysics, epistemology, and ethics, and so the bulk of material included in this volume is on those topics.

3. The first use of the term may be in Heraclitus; it is Plato who tries to restrict the name to a certain group of thinkers.

4. In the 1990s, fragments of a papyrus scroll in Strasbourg were pieced together and discovered to contain text from Empedocles of Acragas. The Strasbourg Papyrus has both known and previously unknown lines, and may well be the only direct transmission of a Presocratic text that we know (although scholars disagree about this). Translations of the new material are included in Chapter 8, Empedocles of Acragas.

In the latter part of the fifth century BCE, there was great interest in social, political, and moral questions, and a number of thinkers explored these topics almost exclusively. They were called Sophists, and they were independent and often itinerant teachers of wisdom and practical political skills. Many of them were accomplished and flamboyant rhetoricians. They investigated questions about the nature of moral virtue and the best way for a city to be governed, taking on paying pupils to whom they taught their rhetorical skills and their social and political views. Most of them were contemporaries of Socrates and some of Plato (who despised them). Aristophanes, the great comic poet, represents Socrates himself as a sophist in *Clouds* (423 BCE, revised 418–416). In the play, the character Socrates has the traditional Presocratic interests in cosmological and meteorological subjects (although in Plato's dialogue *Phaedo*, Socrates stresses that he gave up studying these questions). Moreover, at the same time as philosophy was developing, so was medicine. Ancient medical practitioners were also interested in theory, and in the medical literature (collected in what is called the Hippocratic corpus) there are overlaps with questions and problems that the Presocratics explored. All this suggests that absolute distinctions among Sophists, Medical Practitioners, and Philosophers are too extreme.[5]

In studying the Presocratics, the earliest Greek philosophers, we find ourselves at the beginning of a great intellectual adventure. The metaphysical, epistemological, logical, and ethical problems and puzzles that engaged them became part of the philosophical project that Plato and Aristotle inherited and then passed on to other, later thinkers including ourselves. We may find some of their assumptions and views to be strange, even a bit bizarre, and we may find some of their arguments difficult to comprehend. But these early Greek philosophers understood the importance of sustained rational inquiry and the critical evaluation of arguments and evidence. As we join them in this adventure, we, too, become part of that intellectual tradition that goes back to Miletus.

Sources

No Presocratic book has survived intact, and so what we know of the early Greek philosophers is gathered from other works. The Presocratics

5. There were also religious cults developing during the sixth and fifth centuries BCE that explored questions about human souls and personal identity. See McKirahan for fuller discussions.

were quoted or referred to in many ancient works, ranging from philosophical treatises (e.g., Aristotle and the ancient commentators on Aristotle, or Sextus Empiricus) to works on grammar or entertaining treatises (e.g., Plutarch's "Table-Talk"). Our evidence is of two sorts: direct quotations (often simply called "the fragments") and summaries of Presocratic views, or references to the thinkers and their views (called "testimonia"). One must take care in using the fragments, as the extent of a quotation is often unclear; moreover there can be disagreements about the proper text when more than one source provides a passage. We must also be aware that the sources who quote or refer to our thinkers have their own reasons for doing so: very few are disinterested historians, and so the context may mislead us about the actual view of the philosopher quoted. Because of the fragmentary nature of the evidence, it is important to keep in mind that interpretations are tentative, and based on the best reconstruction of a view that one can offer, using as much evidence as one can. Fuller discussions of these problems may be found in the articles by Mansfeld, Mejer, and Runia, and the book by Osborne found in "Suggestions for Further Reading" at the end of this chapter.

Below is a short list of our most important sources for the Presocratic fragments and testimonia.[6]

Both Plato and Aristotle referred to Presocratic thinkers and occasionally quoted them, but care must be used when dealing with evidence from these sources. Plato and Aristotle used views that they attributed to the earlier philosophers for polemical purposes, and both often gave short summaries of Presocratic positions, which are sometimes inaccurate.

Theophrastus, Eudemus, and Meno were students and associates of Aristotle, and they wrote treatises on the views of earlier thinkers (a project organized by Aristotle). Theophrastus wrote on their theories of perception in his book *On Sensation*, parts of which survive, and on their natural philosophy in a book called *Tenets in Natural Philosophy*. Eudemus concentrated on astronomy, mathematics, and theology, and Meno on medicine. Sadly, except for parts of *On Sensation*, these

---

6. An excellent introduction to the problems of sources may be found in Mansfeld's article, "Doxography of Ancient Philosophy," *The Stanford Encyclopedia of Philosophy (Fall 2008 Edition)*, edited by Edward N. Zalta, which may be found at http://plato.stanford.edu/archives/fall2008/entries/doxography-ancient/.

works are lost and survive only in fragments quoted by later scholars; but where they are available, they can provide important evidence for Presocratic thought.

The Roman orator Cicero (first century BCE) quotes from and refers to the early Greek thinkers in his accounts of philosophy, of which he was a serious student.

Clement of Alexandria (second half of the second century CE) was the author of a work called *Miscellanies*, comparing Greek and Christian thought. In the course of this, he often quotes Presocratic philosophers.

Sextus Empiricus, the skeptical philosopher of the second century CE, quotes many Presocratic views on sense perception and knowledge.

Plutarch, writing in the second century CE, quotes from many of our early Greek philosophers in his numerous essays, collected under the title *Moralia*.

The *Placita* (*Opinions*), a work from the second century CE, also gives information about the Presocratics. Though formerly attributed to Plutarch, it was in fact written by someone else. That person, about whom nothing else is known, is conventionally referred to as pseudo-Plutarch. The *Placita* is based on an earlier lost work, as is *Selections on Natural Philosophy* (*Eclogae Physicae*) by John Stobaeus (fifth century CE). The lost work, by Aëtius, (c.100 CE) was itself based on earlier collections, and probably goes back to Theophrastus.[7]

In the late second or early third century CE, Hippolytus, Bishop of Rome, wrote a book called *Refutation of All Heresies*, in which he argued that Christian heresies can be linked to Greek philosophical thought. In this ambitious work, he gives summaries of Presocratic views and quotes extensively from several of the early Greek philosophers.

Diogenes Laertius (third century CE) produced an entertaining and wide-ranging (but not entirely reliable) work called *Lives of the*

---

7. The history and reconstruction of Aëtius' work is complex and controversial. For a clear discussion see Runia.

Philosophers, drawing on many sources that are now lost. It contains biographical reports, lists of book titles, and summaries of views. Although it was influential in its time, it must be used with caution, as it contains much hearsay and invention.

The Neoplatonist philosopher Simplicius (sixth century CE) wrote detailed commentaries on Aristotle, and his commentary on Book I of Aristotle's *Physics* (in which Aristotle surveyed the views of his predecessors) is a valuable source for Presocratic scholars. In his commentaries, Simplicius provides quotations from a number of important Presocratics, especially Parmenides, Anaxagoras, and Empedocles (in all three cases, Simplicius is the only source for some passages). In the case of Parmenides, Simplicius tells us that he is quoting more of the material than is strictly necessary for his commentary, because copies of Parmenides' work have become rare and ought to be preserved. Alexander of Aphrodisias (c.200 CE) is another such commentator and source, as is Simplicius' contemporary John Philoponus.

Suggestions for Further Reading

Background and General Treatments of the Presocratics

Volumes marked with an asterisk (*) are collections of essays.

Algra, K. 1995. *Concepts of Space in Greek Thought.* Leiden: E. J. Brill.

Barnes, J. 1983. *The Presocratic Philosophers,* 2nd edition. London: Routledge and Kegan Paul.

*Brunschwig, J., and G. E. R. Lloyd. 2000. *Greek Thought: A Guide to Classical Knowledge.* Cambridge, MA: Belknap Press of Harvard University Press.

Burkert, W. "Prehistory of Presocratic Philosophy in an Orientalizing Context." In Curd and Graham, pp. 55–85.

Burnet, J. 1930. *Early Greek Philosophy,* 4th edition. London: Adam and Charles Black.

*Caston, V., and D. Graham, eds. 2002. *Presocratic Philosophy: Essays in Honor of A. P. D. Mourelatos.* Aldershot: Ashgate Publishing Co.

Cherniss, H. 1935. *Aristotle's Criticism of Presocratic Philosophy.* Baltimore: Johns Hopkins Press.

Curd, P. 2008. "Presocratic Philosophy." *The Stanford Encyclopedia of Philosophy (Fall 2008 Edition),* edited by Edward N. Zalta. http://plato.stanford.edu/archives/fall2008/entries/presocratics/.

*Curd, P., and D. H. Graham, eds. 2008. *The Oxford Handbook of Presocratic Philosophy*. New York: Oxford University Press.

*Furley, D. J. 1989. *Cosmic Problems: Essays on Greek and Roman Philosophy of Nature*. Cambridge: Cambridge University Press.

*Furley, D. J., and R. E. Allen, eds. 1970, 1975. *Studies in Presocratic Philosophy*, 2 vols. London: Routledge and Kegan Paul.

*Gill, M. L., and P. Pellegrin, eds. 2006. *A Companion to Ancient Philosophy*. Oxford: Blackwell.

Graham, D. W. 2006. *Explaining the Cosmos: The Ionian Tradition of Scientific Philosophy*. Princeton: Princeton University Press.

Guthrie, W. K. C. 1962, 1965, 1969. *A History of Greek Philosophy*, vols. I, II, and III. Cambridge: Cambridge University Press.

Hussey, E. 1972. *The Presocratics*. London: Duckworth.

*Keyser, P., and Georgia L. Irby-Massie, eds. 2007. *The Routledge Biographical Encyclopedia of Ancient Natural Science*. Oxford: Routledge.

Kirk, G. S., J. E. Raven, and M. Schofield. 1983. *The Presocratic Philosophers*, 2nd edition Cambridge: Cambridge University Press.

*Laks, A., and C. Louguet. 2002. *Qu'est-ce que la Philosophie Présocratique? (What Is Presocratic Philosophy?)* Villeneuve d'Ascq: Presses Universitaires du Septentrion.

*Long, A. A., ed. 1999. *The Cambridge Companion to Early Greek Philosophy*. Cambridge: Cambridge University Press.

Mansfeld, J. "Sources," in Long, pp. 22–44.

*McCoy, J. Forthcoming. *Early Greek Philosophy: Reason at the Beginning of Philosophy*. Washington, DC: The Catholic University of America Press.

McKirahan, R. 2011. *Philosophy Before Socrates*, 2nd edition. Indianapolis: Hackett.

Mejer, J. "Ancient Philosophy and the Doxographic Tradition," in Gill and Pellegrin, pp. 20–33.

*Mourelatos, A. P. D., ed. 1974, 1993. *The Pre-Socratics*. Garden City, NY: Doubleday; reprinted Princeton: Princeton University Press.

Osborne, C. 1987. *Rethinking Early Greek Philosophy: Hippolytus of Rome and the Presocratics*. London: Duckworth.

*Preus, A., ed. 2001. *Before Plato*. Albany: State University of New York Press.

Runia, D. "The Sources for Presocratic Philosophy," in Curd and Graham, pp. 27–54.

Stokes, M. 1971. *One and Many in Presocratic Philosophy*. Washington, DC: The Center for Hellenic Studies.

*Taylor, C. C. W., ed. 1997. *Routledge History of Philosophy, Vol. I: From the Beginning to Plato*. London and New York: Routledge.

*Vlastos, G. 1995. *Studies in Greek Philosophy, Vol. I: The Presocratics,* edited by D. W. Graham. Princeton: Princeton University Press.

Waterfield, R. 2000. *The First Philosophers.* Oxford: Oxford University Press.

West, M. L. 1971. *Early Greek Philosophy and the Orient.* Oxford: Oxford University Press.

*Zeyl, D. 1997. *Encyclopedia of Classical Philosophy.* Westport, CT: Greenwood Press.

2. THE MILESIANS

Thales, Anaximander, and Anaximenes were all from the city of Miletus in Ionia (now the western coast of Turkey) and make up what is referred to as the Milesian "school" of philosophy. Tradition reports that Thales was the teacher of Anaximander, who in turn taught Anaximenes. Aristotle begins his account of the history of philosophy as the search for causes and principles (in Metaphysics I) *with these three.*

2.1. Thales

Thales appears on lists of the seven sages of Greece, a traditional catalog of wise men. The chronicler Apollodorus suggests that he was born around 625 BCE. We should accept this date only with caution, as Apollodorus usually calculated birthdates by assuming that a man was forty years old at the time of his "acme," or greatest achievement. Thus, Apollodorus arrives at the date by assuming that Thales indeed predicted an eclipse in 585 BCE, and was forty at the time. Plato and Aristotle tell stories about Thales that show that even in ancient times philosophers had a mixed reputation for practicality.

1. (11A9) They say that once when Thales was gazing upwards while doing astronomy, he fell into a well, and that a witty and charming Thracian serving-girl made fun of him for being eager to know the things in the heavens but failing to notice what was just behind him and right by his feet.

   (Plato, *Theaetetus* 174a)

2. (11A10) The story goes that when they were reproaching him for his poverty, supposing that philosophy is useless, he learned from his astronomy that the olive crop would be large. Then, while it was still winter, he obtained a little money and made deposits on all the olive presses both in Miletus and in Chios, and since

13

no one bid against him, he rented them cheaply. When the time
came, suddenly many requested the presses all at once, and he
rented them out on whatever terms he wished, and so he made
a great deal of money. In this way he proved that philosophers
can easily be wealthy if they wish, but this is not what they are
interested in.

(Aristotle, *Politics* 1.11 1259a9–18)

*Thales reportedly studied astronomy (there is evidence for his interest in
eclipses, whether or not he had anything to say about the eclipse of 585
BCE), geometry (he was said to have introduced the subject into Greece from
Egypt), and engineering (Herodotus reports that he changed the course of the
Halys river in order to aid the Lydian army). In his account of the cosmos,
Thales reportedly said that the basic stuff was water: This could mean that
everything comes from water as the originating source, or that everything
really is water in one form or another. Aristotle, the source of the reports,
seems unsure about which of these propositions Thales adopted. This shows
that even by Aristotle's time, Thales was probably not known by any direct
written evidence, but only indirectly. According to the tradition that Aristotle
follows, Thales also said that the earth rests or floats on water. Aristotle also
reports that Thales thought that soul produces motion and that a magnetic
lodestone has soul because it causes iron to move.*

3. Thales said that the sun suffers eclipse when the moon comes to
   be in front of it, the day in which the moon produces the eclipse
   being marked by its concealment.

(*P.Oxy.* 53.3710, col. 2, 37–40; not in DK)

4. Causes are spoken of in four ways, of which . . . one is matter. . . .
   Let us take as associates in our task our predecessors who considered the things that are and philosophized about the truth, for it
   is clear that they too speak of certain principles and causes, and so
   it will be useful to our present inquiry to survey them: either we
   will find some other kind of cause or we will be more confident
   about the ones now being discussed.

(Aristotle, *Metaphysics* 1.3 983a26–b6; not in DK)

5. (11A12) Of those who first pursued philosophy, the majority believed that the only principles of all things are principles in the form of matter. For that of which all existing things are composed and that from which they originally come to be and that into which they finally perish—the substance persisting but changing in its attributes—this they state is the element and principle of the things that are. . . . For there must be one or more natures from which the rest come to be, while it is preserved. However, they do not all agree about how many or what kinds of such principles there are, but Thales, the founder of this kind of philosophy, stated it to be water. (This is why he declared that the earth rests on water.) He may have gotten this idea from seeing that the nourishment of all things is moist, and that even the hot itself comes to be from this and lives on this (the principle of all things is that from which they come to be)—getting this idea from this consideration and also because the seeds of all things have a moist nature; and water is the principle of the nature of moist things.

(Aristotle, *Metaphysics* 1.3 983b6–27)

6. (11A14) Some say [the earth] rests on water. This is the oldest account that we have inherited, and they say that Thales of Miletus said this. It rests because it floats like wood or some other such thing (for nothing is by nature such as to rest on air, but on water). He says this just as though the same argument did not apply to the water supporting the earth as to the earth itself!

(Aristotle, *On the Heavens* 2.13 294a28–34; tpc)

7. (11A22) Some say the soul is mixed in with the whole universe, and perhaps this is why Thales supposed that all things are full of gods.

(Aristotle, *On the Soul* 1.5 411a7–8; tpc)

8. (11A22) From what is related about him, it seems that Thales too held that the soul is something productive of motion, if indeed he said that the lodestone has soul, because it moves iron.

(Aristotle, *On the Soul* 1.2 405a19–21; tpc)

2.2. Anaximander

Diogenes Laertius says that Anaximander was sixty-four years old in 547/6 BCE, and this dating agrees with the ancient reports that say that Anaximander was a pupil or follower of Thales. He was said to have been the first person to construct a map of the world, to have set up a gnomon at Sparta, and to have predicted an earthquake. Anaximander makes the originating stuff of the cosmos something indefinite or boundless (apeiron in Greek; later the word can also mean "infinite"). This indefinite stuff is moving, directive of other things, and eternal; thus it qualifies as divine. The apeiron gives rise to something productive of hot and cold, but Anaximander does not say what this "something productive of hot and cold" is. The hot takes the form of fire, the origin of the sun and the other heavenly bodies; while the cold is a dark mist that can be transformed into air and earth. Both air and earth are originally moist, but become drier because of the fire. In the first changes from the originating apeiron, Anaximander postulates substantial opposites (the hot, the cold) that act on one another and that are in turn the generating stuffs for the sensible world. The reciprocal action of the opposites is the subject of B1, the only direct quotation we have from Anaximander (and the extent of the quotation is disputed by scholars). Here he stresses that changes in the world are not capricious, but are ordered; with the mention of justice and retribution he affirms that there are lawlike forces guaranteeing the orderly processes of change between opposites. Anaximander also had theories about the natures of the heavenly bodies and why the earth remains fixed where it is. He made claims about meteorological phenomena, and about the origins of living things, including human beings.

9. (12A9 + 12B1) Of those who declared that the *arkhē*[1] is one, moving and *apeiron*, Anaximander . . . said that the *apeiron* was the *arkhē* and element of things that are, and he was the first to introduce this name for the *arkhē* [that is, he was the first to call the *arkhē apeiron*]. (In addition he said that motion is eternal, in which it occurs that the heavens come to be.) He says that the *arkhē* is neither water nor any of the other things called elements, but some other nature which is *apeiron*, out of which come to be all the heavens and the

1. The word *arkhē* is left untranslated here. It means "originating point" or "first principle."

worlds in them. The things that are perish into the things from which they come to be, according to necessity, for they pay penalty and retribution to each other for their injustice in accordance with the ordering of time, as he says in rather poetical language.

(Simplicius, *Commentary on Aristotle's Physics* 24.13–21)

10. (12A11) He says that the *arkhē* is neither water nor any of the other things called elements, but some nature which is *apeiron*, out of which come to be all the heavens and the worlds in them. This is eternal and ageless and surrounds all the worlds. . . . In addition he said that motion is eternal, in which it occurs that the heavens come to be.

(Hippolytus, *Refutation of All Heresies* 1.6.1–2)

11. (12A15) This [the infinite, *apeiron*] does not have an *arkhē*, but this seems to be the *arkhē* of the rest, and to contain all things and steer all things, as all declare who do not fashion other causes aside from the infinite [the *apeiron*] . . . and this is the divine. For it is deathless and indestructible, as Anaximander and most of the natural philosophers say.

(Aristotle, *Physics* 3.4 203b10–15)

12. (12A10) He declares that what arose from the eternal and is productive of [or, "capable of giving birth to"] hot and cold was separated off at the coming to be of this *kosmos*, and a kind of sphere of flame from this grew around the dark mist about the earth like bark about a tree. When it was broken off and enclosed in certain circles, the sun, moon, and stars came to be.

(Pseudo-Plutarch, *Miscellanies* 2)

13. (12A21) Anaximander says that the sun is equal to the earth, and the circle where it has its vent and on which it is carried is twenty-seven times <the size> of the earth.

(Aëtius 2.21.1)

14. (12A18) Anaximander says that the stars are borne by the circles and spheres on which each one is mounted.

(Aëtius 2.16.5)

15. (12A11) The earth is aloft and is not supported by anything. It stays at rest because its distance from all things is equal. The earth's shape is curved, round, like a stone column. We walk on one of the surfaces and the other one is set opposite. The stars come to be as a circle of fire separated off from the fire in the *kosmos* and enclosed by dark mist. There are vents, certain tube-like passages at which the stars appear. For this reason, eclipses occur when the vents are blocked. The moon appears sometimes waxing, sometimes waning as the passages are blocked or opened. The circle of the sun is twenty-seven times <that of the earth and> that of the moon <eighteen times>, and the sun is highest, and the circles of the fixed stars are lowest. Winds occur when the finest vapors of dark mist are separated off and collect together and then are set in motion. Rain results from the vapor arising from the earth under the influence of the sun. Lightning occurs whenever wind escapes and splits the clouds apart.

(Hippolytus, Refutation of All Heresies 1.6.3–7)

16. (12A23) Anaximander says that these [thunder, lightning, thunderbolts, waterspouts, and hurricanes] all result from wind. For whenever it [wind] is enclosed in a thick cloud and forcibly escapes because it is so fine and light, then the bursting [of the cloud] creates the noise and the splitting creates the flash against the blackness of the cloud.

(Aëtius 3.3.1)

17. (12A26) Some, like Anaximander . . . declare that the earth stays at rest because of equality. For it is no more fitting for what is situated at the center and is equally far from the extremes to move up rather than down or sideways. And it is impossible for it to move in opposite directions at the same time. Therefore, it stays at rest of necessity.

(Aristotle, On the Heavens 2.13 295b11–16)

18. (12A30) Anaximander says that the first animals were produced in moisture, enclosed in thorny barks. When their age advanced they came out onto the drier part, their bark broke off, and they lived a different mode of life for a short time.

(Aëtius 5.19.4)

19. (12A10) He also declares that in the beginning humans were born from animals of a different kind, since other animals quickly manage on their own, and humans alone require lengthy nursing. For this reason they would not have survived if they had been like this at the beginning.

(Pseudo-Plutarch, *Opinions* 2)

20. (12A30) Anaximander . . . believed that there arose from heated water and earth either fish or animals very like fish. In these, humans grew and were kept inside as embryos up to puberty. Then finally they burst, and men and women came forth already able to nourish themselves.

(Censorinus, *On the Day of Birth* 4.7)

2.3. Anaximenes

Ancient sources say that Anaximenes was a younger associate or pupil of Anaximander. Like Anaximander he agrees with Thales that there is a single originative stuff, but he disagrees with both Thales and Anaximander about what it is. He calls this basic stuff aēr *(usually translated "air," although* aēr *is more like a dense mist than what we think of as air, which is ideally transparent). Aēr is indefinite enough to give rise to the other things in the cosmos, but it is not as vague as Anaximander's* apeiron *(or indefinite). Anaximander seems to have left it unclear just what it is that comes from the* apeiron *and then produces the hot and the cold, and Anaximenes could well have argued that the* apeiron *was simply too indefinite to do the cosmic job Anaximander intended for it. In a major step away from Thales and Anaximander, Anaximenes explicitly includes condensation and rarefaction as the processes that transform* aēr *and the other stuffs of the cosmos. Like the other Presocratics, Anaximenes gave explanations of all sorts of meteorological and other natural phenomena.*

21. (13A5) Anaximenes . . . like Anaximander, declares that the underlying nature is one and unlimited [*apeiron*] but not indeterminate, as Anaximander held, but definite, saying that it is air. It differs in rarity and density according to the substances <it becomes>. Becoming finer, it comes to be fire; being condensed, it comes to be wind, then cloud; and when still further condensed, it becomes water, then earth, then stones, and the rest come to be from these. He too makes motion eternal and says that change also comes to be through it.

(Theophrastus, quoted by Simplicius, *Commentary on Aristotle's Physics* 24.26–25.1)

22. (13B2) Just as our soul, being air, holds us together and controls us, so do breath and air surround the whole *kosmos*.

(Pseudo-Plutarch, *Opinions* 876AB)

23. (13A10) Anaximenes determined that air is a god and that it comes to be and is without measure, infinite, and always in motion.

(Cicero, *On the Nature of the Gods* 1.10.26)

24. (13A7) Anaximenes . . . declared that the principle is unlimited [*apeiron*] air, from which come to be things that are coming to be, things that have come to be, and things that will be, and gods and divine things. The rest come to be out of the products of this. The form of air is the following: when it is most even, it is invisible, but it is revealed by the cold and the hot and the wet, and by its motion. It is always moving, for all the things that undergo change would not change if it were not moving. For when it becomes condensed or finer, it appears different. For when it is dissolved into a finer condition it becomes fire, and on the other hand air being condensed becomes winds. Cloud comes from air through felting,[2] and water comes to be when this happens to a greater degree. When condensed still more it becomes earth, and when it reaches the absolutely densest stage it becomes stones.

(Hippolytus, *Refutation of All Heresies* 1.7.1–3)

25. (13B1) Or as Anaximenes of old believed, let us leave neither the cold nor the hot in the category of substance, but <hold them to be> common attributes of matter, which come as the results of its changes. For he declares that the contracted state of matter and the condensed state is cold, whereas what is fine and "loose" (calling

---

2. Translator's note: "Felting" is the production of nonwoven fabric by the application of heat, moisture, and pressure, as felt is produced from wool. The term here is extended to describe any other process in which the product is denser than and so has different properties from the ingredients.

when breathing

it this way with this very word) is hot. As a result he claimed that
it is not said unreasonably that a person releases both hot and cold
from his mouth. For the breath becomes cold when compressed
and condensed by the lips, and when the mouth is relaxed, the
escaping breath becomes warm because of rareness.

(Plutarch, *The Principle of Cold* 7 947F)

26. (13A6) When the air was being felted the earth was the first thing
to come into being, and it is very flat. This is why it rides upon the
air, as is reasonable.

(Pseudo-Plutarch, *Miscellanies* 3)

27. (13A20) Anaximenes, Anaxagoras, and Democritus say that its
flatness is the cause of its staying at rest. For it does not cut the air
below but covers it like a lid, as bodies with flatness apparently
do; they are difficult for winds to move because of their resistance.
They say that the earth does this same thing with respect to the air
beneath because of its flatness. And the air, lacking sufficient room
to move aside, stays at rest in a mass because of the air beneath.

(Aristotle, *On the Heavens* 2.13 294b13–20)

28. (13A7) Likewise the sun and moon and all the other heavenly bodies, which are fiery, ride upon the air on account of their flatness.
The stars came into being from the earth because moisture rises
up out of it. When the moisture becomes fine, fire comes to be and
the stars are formed of fire rising aloft. There are also earthen bodies in the region of the stars carried around together with them.
He says that the stars do not move under the earth as others have
supposed, but around it, as a felt cap turns around our head. The
sun is hidden not because it is under the earth but because it is
covered by the higher parts of the earth and on account of the
greater distance it comes to be from us. Because of their distance
the stars do not give heat.

(Hippolytus, *Refutation of All Heresies* 1.7.4–6)

29. (13A17) Anaximenes stated that clouds occur when the air is further thickened. When it is condensed still more, rain is squeezed
out. Hail occurs when the falling water freezes, and snow when
some wind is caught up in the moisture.

(Aëtius 3.4.1)

30. (13A21) Anaximenes declares that when the earth is being drenched and dried out it bursts, and earthquakes result from these hills breaking off and collapsing. This is why earthquakes occur in droughts and also in heavy rains. For in the droughts, as was said, the earth is broken while being dried out, and when it becomes excessively wet from the waters, it falls apart.

(Aristotle, *Meteorology* 2.7 365b6–12)

Suggestions for Further Reading

The Milesians

All of these entries have further bibliographies; see also the relevant chapters in Barnes and Guthrie. Complete bibliographical information for collections may be found in the bibliography in the Introduction, pp. 10–12.

Algra, K. "The Beginnings of Cosmology," in Long, pp. 45–65.

Gagarin, M. "Greek Law and the Presocratics," in Caston and Graham, pp. 19–24.

Hussey, E. "The Beginnings of Philosophy and Science in Archaic Greece," in Gill and Pellegrin, pp. 3–19.

Kahn, C. H. 1960, 1994. *Anaximander and the Origins of Greek Cosmology*. New York: Columbia University Press; reprint Indianapolis: Hackett.

McKirahan, R. "Anaximander's Infinite Worlds," in Preus, pp. 49–65.

Schofield, M. "The Ionians," in Taylor, pp. 47–87.

White, S. "Milesian Measures: Space, Time, and Matter," in Curd and Graham, pp. 89–133.

————. "Thales and the Stars," in Caston and Graham, pp. 3–18.

3. PYTHAGORAS AND EARLY PYTHAGOREANISM

Pythagoras was born on the island of Samos in the eastern Aegean some time around 570 BCE; according to tradition his father was a gem-cutter or engraver. He reportedly traveled in Egypt and Babylonia, leaving Samos around 530 to escape the rule of the tyrant Polycrates. Eventually, Pythagoras settled in Croton, in southern Italy. There he was well-respected and gained political influence. He founded a community for himself and his followers that was philosophical, political, and religious. The exclusivity of the group angered some, and in about 500 there was an uprising in Croton (and elsewhere in Italy) against the Pythagoreans. The Pythagoreans were temporarily driven out of Croton, and many were killed. Pythagoras himself took refuge in Metapontum and died not long afterwards (some say he starved himself to death in a temple). Despite these and other setbacks—some Pythagoreans departed for the Greek mainland—there continued to be groups of Pythagoreans in southern Italy until about 400. Even then Archytas of Tarentum remained. He was a great mathematician and a friend of Plato.

Little is known of the views of Pythagoras himself, except that he had a reputation for great learning—a reputation that would later be mocked by Heraclitus—and that he was most likely the originator of the important and influential Pythagorean doctrine of the transmigration of souls, a view that Xenophanes ridiculed. This difficulty is noted by those in the ancient world who wrote about Pythagoras (see selection number 8 below). Sometime during his life or after his death, Pythagoras' followers split into two groups, which mirrored the two aspects of Pythagorean teaching. These groups were the mathēmatikoi *and the* akousmatikoi.[1] *The* akousmatikoi *were disciples who venerated Pythagoras' teachings on religion and the proper way to live, but had little interest in the philosophical aspects of*

---

1. The word *akousmatikoi* comes from *akousmata*, "things heard." The word *mathēmatikoi* comes from *mathēmata*, "things studied" or "learned." The later Pythagoreans Philolaus (see Chapter 12) and Archytas (active in the first half of the fourth century) were members of the *mathēmatikoi*. Some scholars think the division belongs to later stages of Pythagoreanism.

Pythagoreanism. The mathēmatikoi *had a great reputation in the ancient world for philosophical, mathematical, musical, and astronomical knowledge, while still following a Pythagorean way of life. All these different branches of study were connected in Pythagorean thought, for the Pythagoreans believed that number was the key to understanding the cosmos. Their original insight seemed to be that the apparent chaos of sound can be brought into rational, hence knowable, order by the imposition of number. They reasoned that the entire universe is a harmonious arrangement* (kosmos *in Greek), ordered by and so knowable through, number. The Pythagoreans apparently rejected the Ionian methods of inquiry, and turned from searching out the basic stuff of the universe to a study of the form that makes it a* kosmos.

Note on the texts: The evidence about Pythagoras and Pythagoreanism is to be found in several chapters in DK. In the texts given here, the first number in parenthesis is the DK number for the chapter in which the passage occurs.

1. (21B7) Once he passed by as a puppy was being beaten,
    the story goes, and in pity said these words:
    "Stop, do not beat him, since it is the soul of a man, a friend
        of mine,
    which I recognized when I heard it crying."
                            (Diogenes Laertius, *Lives of the Philosophers* 8.36)

2. (22B40) Much learning ["polymathy"] does not teach insight. Otherwise it would have taught Hesiod and Pythagoras and moreover Xenophanes and Hecataeus.
                            (Diogenes Laertius, *Lives of the Philosophers* 9.1)

3. (22B129) Pythagoras the son of Mnesarchus practiced inquiry [*historiē*] more than all other men, and making a selection of these writings constructed his own wisdom, polymathy, evil trickery.
                            (Diogenes Laertius, *Lives of the Philosophers* 8.6)

4. (36B4) Thus he [Pherecydes] excelled in both manhood and
        reverence
    and even in death has a delightful life for his soul,
    if indeed Pythagoras was truly wise about all things,

he who truly knew and had learned thoroughly the opinions
of men.[2]

(Diogenes Laertius, *Lives of the Philosophers* 1.120)

5. (31B129) There was a certain man among them who knew very
holy matters,
who possessed the greatest wealth of mind,
mastering all sorts of wise deeds.
For when he reached out with all his mind,
easily he would survey every one of the things that are,
yea, within ten and even twenty generations of humans.[3]

(Porphyry, *Life of Pythagoras* 30)

6. (14,10)[4] Is Homer said to have been during his life a guide in education for people who delighted in associating with him and passed
down to their followers a Homeric way of life? Pythagoras himself
was greatly admired for this, and his followers even nowadays
name a way of life Pythagorean and are conspicuous among
others.

(Plato, *Republic* 10 600a–b)

7. (14,1) The Egyptians were the first to declare this doctrine, too, that
the human soul is immortal, and each time the body perishes it
enters into another animal as it is born. When it has made a circuit
of all terrestrial, marine, and winged animals, it once again enters
a human body as it is born. Its circuit takes three thousand years.
Some Greeks have adopted this doctrine, some earlier and some
later, as if it were peculiar to them.
I know their names, but do not write them.

(Herodotus, *Histories* 2.123)

2. Translator's note: Ion is suggesting that Pherecydes' soul has a delightful
afterlife. Pherecydes lived in the sixth century BCE.

3. This passage is from Empedocles, who does not mention Pythagoras by name
here, and there is doubt (both ancient and modern) whether he meant to praise
Pythagoras here or someone else. (Diogenes Laertius suggested that the verse
was meant to honor Parmenides.)

4. The Pythagoras chapter of DK (14) is not divided into subsections, as are
most of the rest of the chapters; thus there is no indication of "A" or "B" in
references to texts collected there.

8. (14.8a) What he said to his associates, no one is able to say with any certainty, for they kept no ordinary silence among themselves. But it was especially well-known by all that first he declares that the soul is immortal; then that it changes into other kinds of animals; in addition that things that happen recur at certain intervals, that nothing is absolutely new, and that all things that come to be alive must be thought akin. Pythagoras seems to have been the first to introduce these opinions into Greece.

(Porphyry, *Life of Pythagoras* 19)

9. (58B40) Some of them [the Pythagoreans] declared that the soul is the motes in the air, and others that it is what makes the motes move.

(Aristotle, *On the Soul* 1.2 404a17)

10. (14.8) Heraclides of Pontus says that Pythagoras said the following about himself. Once he had been born Aethalides and was believed to be the son of Hermes. When Hermes told him to choose whatever he wanted except immortality, he asked to retain both alive and dead the memory of what happened to him. . . . Afterwards he entered into Euphorbus and was wounded by Menelaus. Euphorbus said that once he had been born as Aethalides and received the gift from Hermes, and told of the migration of his soul and what plants and animals it had belonged to and all it had experienced in Hades. When Euphorbus died his soul entered Hermotimus, who, wishing to provide evidence, went to Branchidae, entered the sanctuary of Apollo, and showed the shield Menelaus had dedicated. (He said that when Menelaus was sailing away from Troy he dedicated the shield to Apollo.) The shield had already rotted away and only the ivory facing was preserved. When Hermotimus died, it [the soul] became Pyrrhus the Delian fisherman and again remembered everything. . . . When Pyrrhus died it became Pythagoras and remembered all that had been said.

(Diogenes Laertius, *Lives of the Philosophers* 8.4–5)

11. (14,2, 58C4) There are two kinds of the Italian philosophy called Pythagorean, since two types of people practiced it—the *akousmatikoi* and the *mathēmatikoi*. Of these, the *akousmatikoi* were admitted to be Pythagoreans by the others, but they, in turn, did not recognize the *mathēmatikoi* but claimed that their pursuits were not those

of Pythagoras, but of Hippasus. . . . The philosophy of the *akousmatikoi* consists of unproved and unargued *akousmata* to the effect that one must act in appropriate ways, and they also try to preserve all the other sayings of Pythagoras as divine dogma. These people claim to say nothing of their own invention and say that to make innovations would be wrong. But they suppose that the wisest of their number are those who have got the most *akousmata*.

(Iamblichus, *Life of Pythagoras* 81, 82; from Aristotle?)

12. (58C4) All the *akousmata* referred to in this way fall under three headings: (a) Some indicate what something is; (b) others indicate what is something in the greatest degree; and (c) others what must or must not be done. (a) The following indicate what something is. What are the Isles of the Blest? Sun and Moon. What is the oracle at Delphi? The tetractys, which is the harmony in which the Sirens sing. (b) Others indicate what is something in the greatest degree. What is most just? To sacrifice. What is the wisest? Number, and second wisest is the person who assigned names to things. What is the wisest thing in our power? Medicine. What is most beautiful? Harmony.

(Iamblichus, *Life of Pythagoras* 82; from Aristotle?)

13. (58C3) <Pythagoras ordered his followers> not to pick up <food> which had fallen, to accustom them not to eat self-indulgently or because it fell on the occasion of someone's death . . . not to touch a white rooster, because it is sacred to the Month and is a suppliant; it is a good thing, and is sacred to the Month because it indicates the hours, and white is of the nature of good, while black is of the nature of evil . . . not to break bread, because friends long ago used to meet over a single loaf just as foreigners still do, and not to divide what brings them together. Others <explain this practice> with reference to the judgment in Hades, others say that it brings cowardice in war, and still others that the whole universe begins from this.

(Aristotle, fr. 195 [Rose], quoted in Diogenes
Laertius, *Lives of the Philosophers* 8.34ff.)

14. (58C6) Do not stir the fire with a knife.
Rub out the mark of a pot in the ashes.
Do not wear a ring.

Do not have swallows in the house.

Spit on your nail parings and hair trimmings.

Roll up your bedclothes on rising and smooth out the imprint of
the body.

Do not urinate facing the sun.

(Selections from Iamblichus, *Protrepticus* 21; from Aristotle?)

15. (14,1) The Egyptians agree in this with those called Orphics . . . and
with the Pythagoreans; for it is likewise unholy for anyone who
takes part in these rites to be buried in woolen garments.

(Herodotus, *Histories* 2.81)

16. The tetractys is a certain number, which being composed of the
four first numbers produces the most perfect number, 10. For 1
and 2 and 3 and 4 come to be 10. This number is the first tetractys
and is called the source of ever-flowing nature, since according
to them the entire *kosmos* is organized according to *harmonia*, and
harmonia is a system of three concords, the fourth, the fifth, and
the octave, and the proportions of these three concords are found
in the aforementioned four numbers.

(Sextus Empiricus, *Against the Mathematicians* 7.94–95; not in DK)

17. (58B4) At the same time as these [Leucippus and Democritus] and,
before them, those called Pythagoreans took hold of mathematics
and were the first to advance that study; and being brought up in
it, they believed that its principles are the principles of all things
that are. Since numbers are naturally first among these, and in
numbers they thought they observed many resemblances to things
that are and that come to be . . . and since they saw the attributes
and ratios of musical scales in numbers, and other things seemed
to be made in the likeness of numbers in their entire nature, and
numbers seemed to be primary in all nature, they supposed the
elements of numbers to be the elements of all things that are.

(Aristotle, *Metaphysics* 1.5 985b23–28; 33–986a2)

18. (58B5)[5] The elements of number are the even and the odd, and of
these the latter is limited and the former unlimited. The one is

5. This material may be based on Aristotle's study of Philolaus, and so it may
refer to the later form of Pythagoreanism developed by Philolaus.

composed of both of these (for it is both even and odd), and number springs from the one; and numbers, as I have said, constitute the whole universe.

(Aristotle, *Metaphysics* 1.5 986a17–21)

19. (58B28) They say that the unlimited is the even. For when this is surrounded and limited by the odd it provides things with the quality of unlimitedness. Evidence of this is what happens with numbers. For when gnomons are placed around the one, and apart, in the one case the shape is always different, and in the other it is always one.

(Aristotle, *Physics* 3.4 203a10–15)

20. (58B5) Others of this same school declare that there are ten principles arranged in parallel columns:

limit	unlimited
odd	even
one	plurality
right	left
male	female
at rest	moving
straight	bent
light	darkness
good	evil
square	oblong

This is how Alcmaeon of Croton too seems to have understood things, and either he took this theory from them or they from him. . . . He says that most human matters are pairs, identifying as the oppositions not definite ones like the Pythagoreans . . . but the Pythagoreans described how many and what the oppositions are.

(Aristotle, *Metaphysics* 1.5 986a22–b2)

Suggestions for Further Reading

All of the entries have further bibliographies. Complete bibliographical information for collections may be found in the bibliography in the Introduction, pp. 10–12. See also the relevant chapters in Barnes; Guthrie; and Kirk, Raven, and Schofield in the Introduction's bibliography.

Barker, A. D. 1989. *Greek Musical Writings, Vol. II: Harmonic and Acoustic Theory.* Cambridge: Cambridge University Press.

Burkert, W. 1972. *Lore and Science in Ancient Pythagoreanism,* translated by E. Minar. Cambridge, MA: Harvard University Press (1st German edition, 1962).

Huffman, C. 1999. "Pythagoras." In *The Stanford Encyclopedia of Philosophy (Winter 2009 Edition),* edited by Edward N. Zalta. http://plato.stanford.edu/archives/win2009/entries/pythagoras/.

———. "The Pythagorean Tradition," in Long, pp. 66–87.

———. 2008. "Pythagoreanism." In *The Stanford Encyclopedia of Philosophy (Fall 2008 Edition),* edited by Edward N. Zalta. http://plato.stanford.edu/archives/fall2008/entries/pythagoreanism/.

———. "Two Problems in Pythagoreanism," in Curd and Graham, pp. 284–304.

———. 2009. "The Pythagorean Conception of the Soul from Pythagoras to Philolaus." In *Body and Soul in Ancient Philosophy,* edited by D. Frede and B. Reis. Berlin: Walter de Gruyter, pp. 21–44.

Hussey, E. "Pythagoreans and Eleatics," in Taylor, pp. 128–74.

Kahn, C. 2001. *Pythagoras and the Pythagoreans.* Indianapolis: Hackett.

Kingsley, Peter. 1995. *Ancient Philosophy, Mystery, and Magic.* Oxford: Clarendon Press.

Minar, Edwin L. 1942. *Early Pythagorean Politics in Practice and Theory.* Baltimore: Waverly Press.

Philip, J. A. 1966. *Pythagoras and Early Pythagoreanism.* Toronto: University of Toronto Press.

Riedweg, Christoph. 2005. *Pythagoras: His Life, Teaching, and Influence.* Ithaca and London: Cornell University Press.

West, M. L. 1992. *Ancient Greek Music.* Oxford: Clarendon Press.

4. XENOPHANES OF COLOPHON

Born in Colophon, a city on the west coast of what is now Turkey, near Miletus (home to Thales, Anaximander, and Anaximenes) and Ephesus (the city of Heraclitus), Xenophanes was an itinerant poet and philosopher. On his own evidence, he lived to a great age, and although the subjects discussed in the surviving fragments and testimonia give evidence of the scope of his travels, the details of his life are hazy. He was born c.570 BCE and seems to have left Colophon after it fell to the Medes in 546/5. He refers to Pythagoras and the doctrine of transmigration of souls in one fragment, and some in the ancient tradition say that he was a teacher of Parmenides (this is most unlikely).

Xenophanes wrote in verse, and while some of the surviving fragments deal with typical poetic topics, he also addressed what would now be called theological and philosophical questions. He rejected the traditional views of the Olympian gods, such as are found in Homer and Hesiod, and claimed that there was a supreme non-anthropomorphic god, who controls the cosmos by thought. Whether or not Xenophanes claimed that there was a single god or only that the supreme god was the greatest of an unnamed number of gods is debated by scholars. He rejected divination and the view that natural phenomena, such as rainbows, have divine significance and claimed that there is no divine communication to human beings. Humans must find out for themselves by inquiry; moreover, Xenophanes raises questions about the possibility of sure and certain knowledge, and suggests that humans must be satisfied with belief or opinion, although he probably thought that this must be backed with evidence. He had a keen interest in the natural world, which is not surprising, given his commitment to inquiry. He noted fossils of sea creatures in the mountains and developed a complicated "cloud astrophysics" to explain the phenomena of the heavens. He argued that the earth is indefinitely broad and extends downwards indefinitely, thus rejecting the view that the sun travels under the earth. Even in "traditional" areas for poets he seems to have held strong views: he gives instructions for a symposium (a drinking party) and laments the over-glorification of athletes. Recent scholarship has come to appreciate Xenophanes as a crucial figure in early Greek thought, whose views on knowledge and the divine were important for later thinkers.

1. (B1) For now the floor is clean, and the hands of all,
   and the cups. One is putting on the woven wreaths,
   another is offering fragrant myrrh in a bowl,
   a mixing bowl stands full of joy,
   another wine, gentle and scented of flowers, is at hand in
      wine-jars   5
   and boasts that it will never betray us.
   In the middle, frankincense is sending forth its holy scent.
   There is cold water sweet and pure.
   Golden loaves of bread are served and a magnificent table
   is laden with cheese and rich honey.   10
   In the center an altar is completely covered in flowers
   and the rooms are full of song and good cheer.
   Cheerful men should first sing a hymn to the god
   with well-omened words and pure speech.
   When they have poured an offering and prayed to be able
      to do acts of justice   15
   (for indeed these are the first things to pray for),
   it is not going too far (*hubris*) if you drink only as much as
      permits you to reach
   home without assistance (unless you are very aged).
   Praise the man who after drinking behaves nobly
   in that he possesses memory and aims for excellence (*aretē*)   20
   and relates neither battles of Titans nor Giants
   nor Centaurs—the fictions of our fathers—
   nor violent conflicts; there is no use in these,
   but it is good always to have high regard for the gods.
                          (Athenaeus, *Scholars at Dinner* 11.462c; tmpc)

2. (B2) If anyone were to achieve a victory
   at Zeus's sanctuary at Olympia by the streams of Pisa
   in a foot race or the pentathlon or in wrestling
   or the painful art of boxing

or the frightful contest they call the pankration,[1]   5
he would be more glorious in the eyes of the citizens.
They would grant him a seat of honor at the games,
he would enjoy meals at public expense
and a gift from the city for his children to inherit.
Even if he were to be victorious with horses he would
   obtain these things.   10
Though he is not as worthy of them as I. For superior to the
   strength
of men or horses is my wisdom.
But these ways are misguided and it is not right
to put strength ahead of wisdom, which is good.
If an excellent boxer were among the people   15
or someone excellent at the pentathlon or in wrestling
or in the foot race (which is the most highly honored
display of strength of all men's deeds in the contests)
that would not make a city be any more in a state of
   eunomia.[2]
A city will find little joy in a person   20
who wins in the contests by the banks of Pisa,
since this does not fatten the city's storerooms.
             (Athenaeus, *Scholars at Dinner* 10.413f)

3. (B7) Once he passed by as a puppy was being beaten,
   the story goes, and in pity said these words:
   "Stop, do not beat him, since it is the soul of a man, a friend
      of mine,
   which I recognized when I heard it crying."
          (Diogenes Laertius, *Lives of the Philosophers* 8.36)

4. (B8) Already there are sixty-seven years
   tossing my speculation throughout the land of Greece,
   and from my birth there were twenty-five in addition to these,
   if indeed I know how to speak truly about these matters.
          (Diogenes Laertius, *Lives of the Philosophers* 9.19)

---

1. *Pankration:* A vicious sport combining boxing, wrestling, and kickboxing.

2. Translator's note: *Eunomia:* the condition in a city where the laws are good and people abide by them.

5. (B10) Ever since the beginning all have learned according
   to Homer . . . .
                          (Herodian, *On Doubtful Syllables* 296.6; tpc)

6. (B11) Both Homer and Hesiod have ascribed to the gods all
   deeds
   which among men are matters of reproach and blame:
   thieving, adultery, and deceiving one another.
                          (Sextus Empiricus, *Against the Mathematicians* 9.193)

7. (B12) . . . as they sang of many illicit acts of the gods
   thieving, adultery, and deceiving one another.
                          (Sextus Empiricus, *Against the Mathematicians* 1.289; tpc)

8. (B14) But mortals suppose that the gods are born,
   have human clothing, and voice, and bodily form.
                          (Clement, *Miscellanies* 5.109)

9. (B15) If horses had hands, or oxen or lions,
   or if they could draw with their hands and produce works as
   men do,
   then horses would draw figures of gods like horses, and oxen
   like oxen,
   and each would render the bodies
   to be of the same frame that each of them have.
                          (Clement, *Miscellanies* 5.110; tpc)

10. (B16) Ethiopians say that their gods are snub-nosed and dark,
   Thracians, that theirs are grey-eyed and red-haired.
                          (Clement, *Miscellanies* 7.22; tpc)

11. (B17) . . . and bacchants [garlands] of pine set around the strong
   house.
                          (Scholium on Aristophanes, *Knights* 408; tpc)

12. (B18) By no means did the gods intimate all things to mortals
   from the beginning,
   but in time, inquiring, they discover better.
                          (Stobaeus, *Selections* 1.8.2; tpc)

13. (B23) One god, greatest among gods and men,
not at all like mortals in form or thought.
(Clement, *Miscellanies*, 5.109; tpc)

14. (B24) . . . whole [he] sees, whole [he] thinks, and whole [he]
hears.
(Sextus Empiricus, *Against the Mathematicians* 9.144; tpc)

15. (B26) . . . always [he] remains in the same [state], changing not
at all,
nor is it fitting that [he] come and go to different places at
different times.
(Simplicius, *Commentary on Aristotle's Physics* 23.10; tpc)

16. (B25) . . . but completely without toil [he] agitates all things by
the will of his mind.
(Simplicius, *Commentary on Aristotle's Physics* 23.19; tpc)

17. (B27) For all things are from the earth and all return to the earth
in the end.
(Theodoretus, *Treatment of Greek Conditions* 4.5)

18. (B28) The earth's upper limit is seen here at our feet,
touching the air. But the lower part goes down without limit.
(Achilles Tatius, *Introduction to the Phaenomena of Aratus* 4.34.11)

19. (B29) All things that come into being and grow are earth and
water.
(John Philoponus, *Commentary on Aristotle's Physics* 1.5.125)

20. (B30) Sea is the source of water and the source of wind.
For not without the wide sea would there come to be
in clouds the force of wind blowing out from within,
nor streams of rivers nor rain water from the sky,
but the great wide sea is the sire of clouds and winds and rivers.
(Geneva Scholium on *Iliad* 21.196)

21. (B31) . . . the sun passing high over the earth and warming it.
(Heraclitus Homericus, *Homeric Allegories* 44.5; tpc)

22. (B32) She whom they call Iris, this too is by nature cloud:
purple, and red, and greeny-yellow to behold.
(Scholium BLT on *Iliad* 11.27; tpc)

23. (B33) We all come into being out of earth and water.
(Sextus Empiricus, *Against the Mathematicians* 10.314)

24. (B34) . . . and of course the clear and certain truth no man has
seen
nor will there be anyone who knows about the gods and what
I say about all things;
for even if, in the best case, someone happened to speak what
has been brought to pass,
nevertheless, he himself would not know, but opinion is
ordained for all.
(Sextus Empiricus, *Against the Mathematicians* 7.49.110; tpc)

25. (B35) Let these things be believed as resembling the truth.
(Plutarch, *Table Talk* 9.7.746b)

26. (B36) . . . however many they have made evident for mortals
to behold.
(Herodian, *On Doubtful Syllables* 296.9)

27. (B38) If god had not fashioned yellow honey, they would say
that figs are far sweeter.
(Herodian, *On Peculiar Speech* 41.5)

28. (A12) Xenophanes used to say that those who say that the gods are
born are just as impious as those who say that they die, since either
way it follows that there is a time when the gods do not exist.
(Aristotle, *Rhetoric* 2.23 1399b6–9)

29. (A30) Some declared the universe to be a single substance . . . not
supposing, like some of the natural philosophers, that what-is
is one, and generating <the universe> out of the one as out of
matter, but speaking differently. For the others add change, since
they generate the universe, but these people say it is unchangeable. . . . Xenophanes, who was the first of these to preach monism
(Parmenides is said to have been his student) made nothing

clear . . . but looking off to the whole heaven he declares that the
one is god.

(Aristotle, *Metaphysics* 1.5 986b10–25)

30. (A32) He says that the sun is gathered together from many small
fires. . . . He declares that the earth is without limit and is not surrounded by air in every direction, that all things come into being
from the earth. And he says that sun and stars come into being
from the clouds.

(Pseudo-Plutarch, *Miscellanies* 4)

31. (A40) The sun <is constituted> out of incandescent clouds.[3]

(Stobaeus, *Opinions* 2.20.3)

32. (A38) <The stars> are constituted out of ignited clouds that die
down every day but become fiery again by night, just like coals.

(Aëtius 2.13.13)

33. (A44) All things of this sort [comets, shooting stars, etc.] are aggre-
gations of incandescent clouds.

(Aëtius 3.2.11)

34. (A33) [Xenophanes] says that the sun comes to be each day from
the gathering together of many small fires, that the earth is unlimited and surrounded by neither the air nor the heavens. There are
unlimited numbers of suns and moons, and everything is from
the earth. He declared that the sea is salty because many mixtures
flow together in it. . . . Xenophanes believes that earth is being
mixed into the sea and over time it is dissolved by the moisture,
saying that he has the following kinds of proofs: sea shells are
found in the middle of earth and in mountains, and imprints of
fish and seals have been found at Syracuse in the quarries, and the
imprint of coral [or, "of a laurel leaf"] in the depth of the stone in
Paros, and on Malta flat impressions of all forms of marine life. He
says that these came about when all things were covered with mud
long ago and the impressions were dried in the mud. All humans
perish when the earth is carried down into the sea and becomes

---

3. Translator's note: The translation of this and the following two passages is
indebted to Mourelatos.

mud, and then there is another beginning of generation, and this change occurs in all the *kosmoi* [that is, in every such cycle].

(Hippolytus, *Refutation of All Heresies* 1.14.3–6)

35. (A39) <Concerning the stars that are called the *Dioscuri*>[4] Xenophanes says that the things like stars that appear on boats are small clouds that glimmer as a result of a certain kind of motion.

(Aëtius 2.18.1)

Suggestions for Further Reading

All of these entries have further bibliographies. Complete bibliographical information for collections may be found in the bibliography in the Introduction, pp. 10–12. See also the relevant chapters in Barnes; McKirahan; Guthrie; and Kirk, Raven, and Schofield.

Classen, C. J. 1989. "Xenophanes and the Tradition of Epic Poetry." In *Ionian Philosophy*, edited by K. J. Boudouris, pp. 91–103. Athens: International Association for Greek Philosophy: International Center for Greek Philosophy and Culture.

Fränkel, H. "Xenophanes' Empiricism and His Theory of Knowledge," in Mourelatos, pp. 118–31. (See Introduction, p. 11.)

Lesher, J. H. 2008. "Xenophanes." In *The Stanford Encyclopedia of Philosophy (Fall 2008 Edition)*, edited by Edward N. Zalta. http://plato.stanford.edu/archives/fall2008/entries/xenophanes/.

———. 1992. *Xenophanes of Colophon: Fragments: A Text and Translation with Commentary*. Toronto: University of Toronto Press. (Greek texts of the fragments; translation, commentary, and notes in English.)

Mourelatos, A. P. D. "The Cloud Astro-Physics of Xenophanes and Ionian Material Monism," in Curd and Graham, pp. 134–68.

4. Translator's note: Literally, "sons of Zeus"; the term was used to refer to Castor and Polydeuces (Pollux). The phenomenon referred to is St. Elmo's Fire.

5. HERACLITUS
OF EPHESUS

According to Diogenes Laertius, Heraclitus of Ephesus was born around 540 BCE. He was a member of one of the aristocratic families of that city, but turned his back on the sort of political life normally associated with persons of rank, ceding his hereditary ruling position to his brother. In the ancient world, he had a reputation for both misanthropy and obscurity—among his traditional nicknames were "the Obscure," and "the Riddler." The reputation is no doubt based on his rude comments about other philosophers, historians, and people in general, the nicknames on the enigmatic paradoxes he uses to present his views. He is said to have written a single book, of which fragment 1 was likely the beginning (or very near the beginning).

Although Heraclitus has cosmological views, many of which seem to have been influenced by Xenophanes, he is as interested in exploring questions about knowledge, the soul, and the human condition as in making claims about the physical world. He asserted that a single divine law controls and steers the cosmos. He calls this the logos. The word logos means, among other things, "account," or "thing said," or even "word." As with the English word "account," to give a logos is to say something, but also to give an explanation. Heraclitus is well aware of the ambiguities and complications possible in the words he uses, and he takes full advantage of the flexibility of the Greek language to make multiple points. Although the logos is an objective and independent truth available to all, Heraclitus is convinced that most people do not exercise the capacities required to come to understand it, and instead act like dreamers asleep in their own private worlds. Treating the logos as the divine law of the cosmos, the content of which is a truth to be grasped by humans who can (with difficulty) come to understand the cosmos, Heraclitus attempts to bridge the gap between divine and human knowledge pointed out by Homer, Hesiod, and Alcmaeon. The soul that understands the logos can, apparently, have the sure and certain knowledge that Xenophanes claimed "no man has seen." The path to this understanding is not, Heraclitus thinks, just the inquiry recommended by Xenophanes: Heraclitus ridicules those who have much learning but little understanding. The accumulation of facts without insight into the divine law-like workings of the cosmos is useless. Understanding how all things form a unity is a fundamental part of the necessary insight. Heraclitus offers signs of this unity in his paradoxical claims about the identity of opposites, insisting that despite unceasing change in the cosmos, there is an unchanging principle—the logos—*that both governs and explains these changes. The physical sign of the* logos *is fire: always changing yet always the same.*

Note on the order of the fragments: Sextus Empiricus, our source for the first two fragments, says that they occurred at or near the beginning of Heraclitus' book, but we do not have similar information for the rest of the fragments. Their ordering is a controversial issue, as a particular order can impose an interpretation. In DK the fragments are ordered alphabetically by the name of the source. Here, the fragments are grouped more or less thematically, beginning with B1 and B2, and then going on to some general comments about the inadequacies of other thinkers and ordinary people. There are then observations on the difficulty of learning about the *logos,* but also encouraging remarks suggesting that proper thinking can lead people to the truth contained in the *logos.* There follow claims about the content of the *logos,* opposition and the unity of opposites, and the cosmos. Finally, there are fragments on soul, the human condition, and some remarks on religion. The reader should keep in mind that most Heraclitean sentences address several philosophical problems, and can be relevant for making a number of philosophical points. Fragments whose authenticity is disputed are marked with an asterisk (*).

1. (22B1) Although this *logos* holds always humans prove unable to understand it both before hearing it and when they have first heard it. For although all things come to be [or, "happen"] in accordance with this *logos,* humans are like the inexperienced when they experience such words and deeds as I set out, distinguishing each thing in accordance with its nature (*physis*) and saying how it is. But other people fail to notice what they do when awake, just as they forget what they do while asleep.

   (Sextus Empiricus, *Against the Mathematicians* 7.132)

2. (B2) For this reason it is necessary to follow what is common. But although the *logos* is common, most people live as if they had their own private understanding.

(Sextus Empiricus, *Against the Mathematicians* 7.133)

3. (B40) Much learning ["polymathy"] does not teach insight. Otherwise it would have taught Hesiod and Pythagoras and moreover Xenophanes and Hecataeus.

(Diogenes Laertius, *Lives of the Philosophers* 9.1)

4. (B129) Pythagoras the son of Mnesarchus practiced inquiry [*historiē*] more than all other men, and making a selection of these writings constructed his own wisdom, polymathy, evil trickery.

(Diogenes Laertius, *Lives of the Philosophers* 8.6)

5. (B42) Heraclitus said that Homer deserved to be expelled from the contests and flogged, and Archilochus likewise.

(Diogenes Laertius, *Lives of the Philosophers* 9.1)

6. (B39) In Priene was born Bias, son of Teutames, whose worth (*logos*) is greater than the others'.

(Diogenes Laertius, *Lives of the Philosophers* 1.88)

7. (B57) Most men's teacher is Hesiod. They are sure he knew most things—a man who could not recognize day and night; for they are one.[1]

(Hippolytus, *Refutation of All Heresies* 9.10.2)

8. (B104) What understanding (*noos*) or intelligence (*phrēn*) have they? They put their trust in popular bards and take the mob for their teacher, unaware that most people are bad, and few are good.

(Proclus, *Commentary on Plato's Alcibiades I* 117, Westerink)

9. (B86) Divine things for the most part escape recognition because of unbelief.

(Plutarch, *Life of Coriolanus* 38 = Clement, *Miscellanies* 5.88.4)

---

1. Translator's note: The verbs translated "are sure," "knew," and "recognize" are almost synonyms and can all be translated as "know," a translation that would emphasize the paradoxical suggestion of the fragment.

10. (B108) Of all those whose accounts (*logoi*) I have heard, no one reaches the point of recognizing that what is wise is set apart from all.

(Stobaeus, *Selections* 3.1.174)

11. (B50) Listening not to me, but to the *logos*, it is wise to agree that all things are one.

(Hippolytus, *Refutation of All Heresies* 9.9.1)

12. (B123) Nature (*physis*) loves to hide.

(Themistius, *Orations* 5.69)

13. (B107) Eyes and ears are bad witnesses to people if they have barbarian[2] souls.

(Sextus Empiricus, *Against the Mathematicians* 7.126)

14.* (B46) [He said that] conceit is a holy disease[3] [and that] sight tells falsehoods.

(Diogenes Laertius, *Lives of the Philosophers* 9.7)

15. (B34) Uncomprehending when having heard, they are like the deaf. The saying describes them: being present they are absent.

(Clement, *Miscellanies* 5.115.3; tpc)

16. (B93) The Lord whose oracle is at Delphi neither speaks nor conceals but gives a sign.

(Plutarch, *On the Pythian Oracle* 404D)

17. (B113) Thinking (*phronein*) is common to all.

(Stobaeus, *Selections* 3.1.179)

18. (B112) Right thinking (*sōphronein*) is the greatest excellence, and wisdom (*sophia*) is to speak the truth and act in accordance with nature (*physis*) while paying attention to it.

(Stobaeus, *Selections* 3.1.178)

2. Translator's note: A *barbaros* was originally anyone who did not speak Greek. . . . Heraclitus . . . uses the word here of people who do not understand the *logos*.

3. Translator's note: A reference to epilepsy, which was called the holy disease.

19. * (B73) One ought not to act and speak like people asleep.
(Marcus Aurelius, *Meditations* 4.43)

20. (B89) For the waking there is one common world, but when asleep each person turns away to a private one.
(Pseudo-Plutarch, *On Superstition* 166c)

21. (B26) A man in the night kindles a light for himself when his sight is extinguished; living he touches[4] the dead when asleep, when awake he touches the sleeper.
(Clement, *Miscellanies* 4.141.2)

22. (B21) What we see when awake is death, what we see asleep is sleep.
(Clement, *Miscellanies* 3.21.1)

23. (B114) Those who speak with understanding (*noos*) must rely firmly on what is common to all as a city must rely on [its?] law, and much more firmly. For all human laws are nourished by one law, the divine law; for it has as much power as it wishes and is sufficient for all and is still left over.
(Stobaeus, *Selections* 3.1.179)

24. (B18) Unless he hopes for the unhoped for, he will not find it, since it is not to be hunted out and is impassable (*aporon*).[5]
(Clement, *Miscellanies* 2.17.4)

25. (B22) Those who seek gold dig up much earth but find little.
(Clement, *Miscellanies* 4.4.2)

26. (B17) For many, in fact all that come upon them, do not understand such things, nor when they have noticed them do they know them, but they seem to themselves <to do so>.
(Clement, *Miscellanies* 2.8.1)

---

4. Translator's note: The Greek word for "kindles" and "touches" is the same.
5. Translator's note: *aporon* ("without a path") is related to *aporia* ("perplexity").

27. * (B72) They are at odds with the *logos,* with which above all they are in continuous contact, and the things they meet every day appear strange to them.

(Marcus Aurelius, *Meditations* 4.46)

28. * (B70) [Heraclitus judged human opinions to be] children's playthings.

(Stobaeus, *Selections* 2.1.16)

29. (B19) [Rebuking some for their unbelief, Heraclitus says,] Knowing neither how to hear nor how to speak.

(Clement, *Miscellanies,* 2.24.5)

30. (B28) The knowledge of the most famous persons, which they guard, is but opinion. . . . Justice will convict those who fabricate falsehoods and bear witness to them.

(Clement, *Miscellanies* 5.9.3)

31. (B87) A fool is excited by every word (*logos*).

(Plutarch, *On Listening to Lectures* 40f–41a)

32. (B97) Dogs bark at everyone they do not know.

(Plutarch, *Should Old Men Take Part in Politics?* 787c)

33. (B56) People are deceived about the knowledge of obvious things, like Homer, who was wiser than all the Greeks. For children who were killing lice deceived him by saying, "All we saw and caught we have left behind, but all we neither saw nor caught we bring with us."

(Hippolytus, *Refutation of All Heresies* 9.9.5)

34. (B47) Let us not make random conjectures about the greatest matters.

(Diogenes Laertius, *Lives of the Philosophers* 9.73)

35. (B116) It belongs to all people to know themselves and to think rightly (*sōphronein*).

(Stobaeus, *Selections* 3.5.6)

36. (B35) Men who are lovers of wisdom must be inquirers into many things indeed.

(Clement, *Miscellanies* 5.140.5)

37. (B101) I searched [or: inquired into] myself.

(Plutarch, *Against Colotes* 1118C)

38. (B54) An unapparent connection (*harmonia*) is stronger than an apparent one.

(Hippolytus, *Refutation of All Heresies* 9.9.5)

39. (B12) Upon those who step into the same rivers, different and again different waters flow.

(Arius Didymus, fr. 39.2 = *Dox. Gr.* 471.4–5)

40. (B91) [It is not possible to step twice into the same river]. . . . It scatters and again comes together, and approaches and recedes.

(Plutarch, *On the E at Delphi* 392b)

41.* (B49a) We step into and we do not step into the same rivers. We are and we are not.

(Heraclitus Homericus, *Homeric Questions* 24)

42. (B78) Human nature has no insight, but divine nature has it.

(Origen, *Against Celsus* 6.12)

43. (B45) You would not discover the limits of the soul although you traveled every road: so deep a *logos* does it have.

(Diogenes Laertius, *Lives of the Philosophers* 9.7)

44.* (B115) The soul has a self-increasing *logos*.

(Stobaeus, *Selections* 3.1.180)

45. (B30) This *kosmos,* the same for all, none of gods nor humans made, but it was always and is and shall be: an ever-living fire, kindled in measures and extinguished in measures.

(Clement, *Miscellanies* 5.103.3; tpc)

46. (B41) The wise is one (*to sophon*), to know the intelligent plan (*gnōmē*) by which all things are steered through all.

(Diogenes Laertius, *Lives of the Philosophers* 9.1; tpc)

47. (B32) The wise (*to sophon*) is one alone, both unwilling and willing to be called by the name of Zeus.

(Clement, *Miscellanies* 5.115.1; tpc)

48. (B64) Thunderbolt steers all things.

(Hippolytus, *Refutation of All Heresies* 9.10.7)

49. (B90) All things are an exchange for fire and fire for all things, as goods for gold and gold for goods.

(Plutarch, *On the E at Delphi* 338d–e)

50. (B65) Fire is want and satiety.

(Hippolytus, *Refutation of All Heresies* 9.10.7)

51.* (B76) Fire lives the death of earth and *aēr* lives the death of fire, water lives the death of *aēr*, earth that of water.

(Maximus of Tyre, 41.4)

52. (B36) For souls to become water is to die; for water to become earth is to die; but from earth, water comes to be; from water, soul.

(Clement, *Miscellanies* 6.17.2; tpc)

53. (B118) Gleam of light: the dry soul, wisest (*sophōtate*) and best.

(Stobaeus, *Selections* 3.5.8)

54. (B117) A man when drunk is led by a boy, stumbling and not knowing where he goes, since his soul is moist.

(Stobaeus, *Selections* 3.5.7)

55. (B84a) Changing it rests.

(Plotinus, *Enneads* 4.8.1)

56. (B125) Even the *Kykeōn* [posset][6] falls apart if it is not stirred.

(Theophrastus, *On Vertigo* 9; tpc)

6. The *Kykeōn* is a potion made of ground barley, grated cheese, and wine (sometimes with honey).

57. (B80) It is necessary to know that war is common and justice is strife and that all things happen in accordance with strife and necessity.

(Origen, *Against Celsus* 6.42)

58. (B53) War is the father of all and king of all, and some he shows as gods, others as humans; some he makes slaves, others free.

(Hippolytus, *Refutation of All Heresies* 9.9.4)

59. (B8) What is opposed brings together; the finest harmony [*harmonia*] is composed of things at variance, and everything comes to be [or, "occurs"] in accordance with strife. conflict

(Aristotle, *Nicomachean Ethics* 8.2 1155b4)

60. (B10) Things taken together are whole and not whole, <something that is> being brought together and brought apart, in tune and out of tune; out of all things there comes a unity and out of a unity all things.

([Aristotle], *On the World* 5 396b20)

61. (B51) They do not understand how, though at variance with itself, it agrees with itself.[7] It is a backwards-turning[8] attunement like that of the bow and lyre.

(Hippolytus, *Refutation of All Heresies* 9.9.2)

62. (B55) All that can be seen, heard, experienced—these are what I prefer.

(Hippolytus, *Refutation of All Heresies* 9.9.5)

63. (B101a) Eyes are more accurate witnesses than the ears.

(Polybius, *Histories* 12.27.1)

64. (B7) If all things were smoke, nostrils would distinguish them.

(Aristotle, *On the Senses and Their Objects* 5 443a23)

---

7. Translator's note: Or, "how by being at variance with itself it agrees with itself"; more literally, "how (by) being brought apart it is brought together."

8. Reading *palintropos* here. Translator's note: The sources disagree; some give *palintonos*, "backwards-stretching." There is no scholarly consensus on which word Heraclitus used.

65. (B98) Souls [have use of the sense of] smell in Hades.

(Plutarch, *On the Face in the Moon* 943E)

66. (B48) The name of the bow is life, but its work is death.[9]

(*Etymologium Magnum* sv *bios*)

67. (B59) The track of writing [or, "the path of the carding wheels"][10] is straight and crooked.

(Hippolytus, *Refutation of All Heresies* 9.10.4)

68. (B60) The road up and the road down are one and the same.

(Hippolytus, *Refutation of All Heresies* 9.10.4)

69. (B61) The sea is the purest and most polluted water: to fishes drinkable and bringing safety, to humans undrinkable and destructive.

(Hippolytus, *Refutation of All Heresies* 9.10.5)

70.* (B82) The most beautiful of apes is ugly in comparison with the human race.

(Plato, *Hippias Major* 289a3–4)

71. (B13) Pigs rejoice in mud more than in pure water.

(Clement, *Miscellanies* 1.2.2)

72. (B9) Asses would choose rubbish rather than gold.

(Aristotle, *Nicomachean Ethics* 10.5 1176a7)

73. (B4) We would call oxen happy when they find bitter vetch to eat.

(Albertus Magnus, *On Vegetables* 6.401)

---

9. Translator's note: The fragment exploits the identical spelling of the Greek words for bow (*biós*) and life (*bíos*); they differed in the accented syllables, but in Heraclitus' time accents were not yet written. Also, the fragment does not contain the word *biós* (bow), but uses the more common word *toxon*, thus requiring Heraclitus' readers (or hearers) to make the essential association themselves.

10. Translator's note: The manuscript reading *gnapheiōn* ("carding wheels") is emended by some editors to *grapheiōn* ("writing").

74. (B37) Pigs wash themselves in mud, birds in dust or ash.

(Columella, *On Agriculture* 8.4.4)

75. (B11) Every beast is driven to pasture by blows.

([Aristotle], *On the World* 6 401a10)

76. (B83) The wisest of humans will appear as an ape in comparison with a god in respect to wisdom, beauty, and all other things.

(Plato, *Hippias Major* 289b4–5)

77. (B102) To god all things are beautiful and good and just, but humans have supposed some unjust and others just.

(Porphyry, *Notes on Homer*, on *Iliad* 4.4)

78. (B124) The most beautiful *kosmos* is a pile of things poured out at random.

(Theophrastus, *Metaphysics* 15)

79. (B103) The beginning and the end are common on the circumference of a circle.

(Porphyry, *Notes on Homer*, on *Iliad* 24.200)

80. (B126) Cold things grow hot, a hot thing cold, a moist thing withers, a parched thing is moistened.

(John Tzetzes, *Notes on the Iliad*, p. 126 Hermann)

81. (B67) God is day and night, winter and summer, war and peace, satiety and hunger, but changes the way <fire,(?)> when mingled with perfumes, is named according to the scent of each.

(Hippolytus, *Refutation of All Heresies* 9.10.8)

82. (B88) The same thing is both living and dead, and the waking and the sleeping, and young and old; for these things transformed are those, and those transformed back again are these.

(Pseudo-Plutarch, *Consolation to Apollonius* 106E)

83. (B23) They would not have known the name of justice if these things [unjust things] did not exist.

(Clement, *Miscellanies* 4.9.7)

84. (B111) Disease makes health pleasant and good, hunger satiety, weariness rest.

(Stobaeus, *Selections* 3.1.178)

85. (B58) Physicians who cut and burn complain that they receive no worthy pay, although they do these things.

(Hippolytus, *Refutation of All Heresies* 9.10.3)

86. (B62) Immortal mortals, mortal immortals, living the death of the others and dying their life.

(Hippolytus, *Refutation of All Heresies* 9.10.6)

87. (B31) The turnings of fire: first, sea; and of sea, half is earth and half fiery waterspout. . . . Earth is poured out as sea, and is measured according to the same ratio (*logos*) it was before it became earth.

(Clement, *Miscellanies* 5.104 3,5)

88. (B3 + B94) The sun by its nature is the width of a human foot, not exceeding in size the limits of its width . . . Otherwise, the Erinyes, ministers of Justice, will find him out.

(Derveni Papyrus, col. IV)

89. (B6) The sun is new each day.

(Aristotle, *Meteorology* 2.2 355a13)

90. (B99) If there were no sun, as far as concerns all the other stars[11] it would be night.

(Plutarch, *Is Water or Fire the More Useful?* 957A)

91. (B120) Limits of dawn and evening are the Bear and opposite the Bear,[12] the limit of bright Zeus.

(Strabo, *Geography* 1.6)

11. Translator's note: The clause "as far . . . stars" is omitted in one of the sources and may not be authentic.

12. Translator's note: The Bear is the constellation Ursa Major (the Big Dipper), and "opposite the Bear" refers to the star Arcturus, which was used as an indicator of the seasons.

92. (B136) Souls slain in war are purer than those that perish of diseases.

(Bodleian Scholium on Epictetus, lxxi Schenkel)

93. (B24) Gods and humans honor those slain in war.

(Clement, *Miscellanies* 4.16.1)

94. (B25) Greater deaths win greater destinies.

(Clement, *Miscellanies* 4.49.2)

95. (B27) Things unexpected and unthought of await humans when they die.

(Clement, *Miscellanies* 4.22.144)

96. (B63) They arise and become vigilant guardians of the living and the dead.

(Hippolytus, *Refutation of All Heresies* 9.10.6)

97. (B20) When they are born, they are willing to live and to have their destinies, and they leave children behind to become their destinies.

(Clement, *Miscellanies* 3.14.1)

98. (B16) How could one fail to be seen by that which does not set?

(Clement, *Pedagogue* 2.99.5)

99. (B96) Corpses are more fit to be thrown out than dung.

(Plutarch, *Table Talk* 669A)

100. (B121) Every grown man of the Ephesians should hang himself and leave the city to the boys; for they banished Hermodorus, the best man among them, saying "let no one of us excel, or if he does, be it elsewhere and among others."

(Strabo, *Geography* 14.25)

101. (B125a) May wealth never leave you, Ephesians, lest your wickedness be revealed.

(John Tzetzes, Scholium on Aristophanes' *Wealth* 88)

102. (B49) One person is ten thousand to me if he is best.

(Theodorus Prodromus, *Letters* 1)

103. (B52) A lifetime is a child playing, playing checkers; the kingdom belongs to a child.

(Hippolytus, *Refutation of All Heresies* 9.94)

104. (B44) The people must fight for the law as for the city wall.

(Diogenes Laertius, *Lives of the Philosophers* 9.2)

105. (B43) Willful violence [*hubris*] must be quenched more than a fire.

(Diogenes Laertius, *Lives of the Philosophers* 9.3)

106. (B119) A person's character is his divinity [or, "guardian spirit," *daimōn*].

(Stobaeus, *Selections* 4.40.23)

107. (B110) It is not better for humans to get all they want.

(Stobaeus, *Selections* 3.1.176)

108. (B95) It is better to conceal ignorance.

(Plutarch, *Table Talk* 644F)

109. (B85) It is difficult to fight against anger, for whatever it wants it buys at the price of the soul.

(Plutarch, *Life of Coriolanus* 22.2)

110. (B5) They vainly purify themselves with blood when defiled with it, as if a man who had stepped into mud were to wash it off with mud. He would be thought mad if anyone noticed him acting thus.

(Aristocritus, *Theosophia* 68; Origen, *Against Celsus* 7.62)

111. (B15) If it were not for Dionysus that they hold processions and sing hymns to the shameful parts [*phalli*], it would be a most shameless act; but Hades and Dionysus are the same, in whose honor they go mad and celebrate the Bacchic rites.

(Clement, *Protreptic* 34.5)

112. (B14) Nightwalkers, Magi, Bacchoi, Lenai, and the initiated. [These people Heraclitus threatens with what happens after death. . . .]

For the secret rites practiced among humans are celebrated in an unholy manner.

(Clement, *Protreptic* 22)

113. (B92) The Sibyl with raving mouth uttering mirthless [and unadorned and unperfumed phrases, reaches a thousand years in her voice on account of the god].[13]

(Plutarch, *On the Oracles at Delphi* 397A)

Suggestions for Further Reading

All of these entries have further bibliographies. Complete bibliographical information for collections may be found in the bibliography in the Introduction, pp. 10–12. See also the relevant chapters in Barnes; Guthrie; McKirahan; and Kirk, Raven, and Schofield.

Betegh, G. 2007. "On the Physical Aspect of Heraclitus' Psychology." *Phronesis* 52: pp. 3–32.

Dilcher, R. 1995. *Studies in Heraclitus*. Hildesheim: Georg Olms.

Graham, D. W. 2006. *Explaining the Cosmos: The Ionian Tradition of Scientific Philosophy*. Princeton: Princeton University Press.

———. 2008. "Heraclitus." In *The Stanford Encyclopedia of Philosophy (Fall 2008 Edition)*, edited by Edward N. Zalta. http://plato.stanford.edu/archives/fall2008/entries/heraclitus/.

———. "Heraclitus: Flux, Order, and Knowledge," in Curd and Graham, pp. 169–88.

Hussey, E. 1982. "Epistemology and Meaning in Heraclitus." In *Language and Logos*, edited by M. Schofield and M. Nussbaum, pp. 33–59. Cambridge: Cambridge University Press.

———. "Heraclitus," in Long, pp. 88–112.

Kahn, C. H. 1979. *The Art and Thought of Heraclitus*. Cambridge: Cambridge University Press.

Kirk, G. S. 1954. *Heraclitus: The Cosmic Fragments*. Cambridge: Cambridge University Press.

Marcovich, Miroslav. 1967, 2001. *Heraclitus*. Mérida, Venezuela: University of the Andes Press; 2nd edition, Sankt Augustin: Academia Verlag.

13. Translator's note: The bracketed material may contain Heraclitean ideas, although the wording is probably not authentic.

Nehamas, A. 2002. "Parmenidean Being/Heraclitean Fire." In *Presocratic Philosophy: Essays in Honour of Alexander Mourelatos,* edited by V. Caston and D. W. Graham, pp. 45–64. Aldershot: Ashgate.

Nussbaum, M. C. 1972. "*Psyche* in Heraclitus." *Phronesis* 17: pp. 1–16; 153–70.

Osborne, C. "Heraclitus," in Taylor, pp. 88–127.

Robinson, T. M. 1987. *Heraclitus.* Toronto: University of Toronto Press.

Vlastos, G. 1955. "On Heraclitus." *American Journal of Philology* 76: pp. 337–78; reprinted in Vlastos, *Studies in Greek Philosophy, Vol. I: The Presocratics,* edited by D. W. Graham, pp. 127–50.

6. PARMENIDES OF ELEA

The most reliable reports on the life of Parmenides of Elea (an Italian town today called Velia near what is now Naples) imply that he was born around 515 BCE. Diogenes Laertius says that he was a pupil of Xenophanes, "but did not follow him" (i.e., he did not adopt Xenophanes' views). Diogenes Laertius also says that Parmenides was, at some time in his life associated with the Pythagoreans. There is no way of knowing whether or not these reports are true, but it seems clear that Parmenides is concerned with answering questions about knowledge that are generated by Xenophanes' views. (It is less clear that, as sometimes claimed, Xenophanes' account of his greatest god [see Chapter 4 fragment 13] influenced Parmenides' account of what-is.) It would not be surprising that Parmenides should know about Pythagoreanism, as Elea is in the southern part of Italy, which was home to the Pythagorean movement.

Like Xenophanes, Parmenides wrote in verse: His poem is in Homeric hexameters, and there are many Homeric images, especially from the Odyssey. In the poem Parmenides presents a young man (kouros, in Greek), who is taken in a chariot to meet a goddess. He is told by her that he will learn "all things"; moreover, while the goddess says that what the kouros is told is true, she stresses that he himself must test and assess the arguments she gives. Parmenides is one of the most important and most controversial figures among the early Greek thinkers, and there is much disagreement among scholars about the details of his views. The poem begins with a long introduction (The Proem, B1); this is followed by a section traditionally called Truth (B2–B8.50). This is followed by the so-called Doxa section ("beliefs" or "opinions")—a cosmology that, the goddess warns, is in some way deceptive. In Truth, Parmenides argues that genuine thought and knowledge can only be about what genuinely is (what-is), for what-is-not is literally unsayable and unthinkable. Parmenides warns against what he calls the "beliefs of mortals," based entirely on sense-experience; in these, the goddess says, "there is no true trust." Rather, one must judge by understanding (the capacity to reason) what follows from the basic claim that what-is must be, and what-is-not cannot be. The poem proceeds (in the

*crucial fragment B8) to explore the features of genuine being: What-is must
be whole, complete, unchanging, and one. It can neither come to be nor pass
away, nor undergo any qualitative change. Only what is in this way can be
grasped by thought and genuinely known.*

*Given these arguments, the accounts of the way things are given by
Parmenides' predecessors cannot be acceptable. The earlier views required
fundamental changes in their theoretically basic entities, or relied on
the reality of opposites and their unity; Parmenides argues that all these
presuppose the reality of what-is-not, and so cannot succeed. For modern
scholars, one particularly intriguing aspect of Parmenides' thought is that,
having apparently rejected the world of sensory experience as unreal, the
goddess then goes on, in the Doxa, to give a cosmological account of her
own. Is this meant to be a parody of other views? Is it the best that can be
said for the world that appears to human senses? Is it a lesson for the hearer,
to test whether any cosmology could ever be acceptable on Parmenidean
grounds? There is little agreement among Parmenides' readers on this.
While Parmenides clearly shares with Xenophanes and Heraclitus interests
in metaphysical and epistemological questions, Parmenides is the first to
see the importance of metatheoretical questions about philosophical theories
themselves, and to provide comprehensive arguments for his claims. These
arguments are powerful, and Parmenides' views about knowledge, being,
and change were a serious theoretical challenge, not only to later Presocratic
thinkers, but also to Plato and Aristotle.*

1. (28B1) The mares which carry me as far as my spirit ever
        aspired
    were escorting me, when they brought me and proceeded
        along the renowned route
    of the goddess, which brings a knowing mortal to all cities
        one by one.
    On this route I was being brought, on it wise mares were
        bringing me,
    straining the chariot, and maidens were guiding the way.   5
    The axle in the center of the wheel was shrilling forth the
        bright sound of a musical pipe,
    ablaze, for it was being driven forward by two rounded
    wheels at either end, as the daughters of the Sun

were hastening to escort \<me\> after leaving the house of
   Night
for the light, having pushed back the veils from their heads
   with their hands.   10
There are the gates of the roads of Night and Day,
and a lintel and a stone threshold contain them.
High in the sky they are filled by huge doors
of which avenging Justice holds the keys that fit them.
The maidens beguiled her with soft words   15
and skillfully persuaded her to push back the bar for them
quickly from the gates. They made
a gaping gap of the doors when they opened them,
swinging in turn in their sockets the bronze posts
fastened with bolts and rivets. There, straight through them
   then,   20
the maidens held the chariot and horses on the broad road.
And the goddess received me kindly, took my
right hand in hers, and addressed me with these words:
Young man, accompanied by immortal charioteers,
who reach my house by the horses which bring you,   25
welcome—since it was not an evil destiny that sent you
   forth to travel
this route (for indeed it is far from the beaten path of
   humans),
but Right and Justice. It is right that you learn all things—
both the unshaken heart of well-persuasive[1] Truth
and the beliefs of mortals, in which there is no true trust.   30
But nevertheless you will learn these too—how it were
   right that the things that seem
be reliably, being indeed, the whole of things.

> (lines 1–30: Sextus Empiricus, *Against the Mathematicians*
> 7.111–14; lines 28–32: Simplicius, *Commentary on
> Aristotle's On the Heavens,* 557.25–558.2; tmpc)

2. (B2) But come now, I will tell you—and you, when you have
   heard the story, bring it safely away—
which are the only routes of inquiry that are for thinking:

---

1. The manuscript text of this word varies; another reading is translated "well-
rounded Truth."

(handwritten margin note at top: "why refer to something there isn't anything to refer to")

(handwritten margin note left: "path of persuasion")

the one, that is and that it is not possible for it not to be,
is the path of Persuasion (for it attends upon Truth),
the other, that it is not and that it is right that it not be,   5
this indeed I declare to you to be a path entirely unable to
    be investigated:

(handwritten margin note left: "can know what is")

For neither can you know what is not (for it is not to be
    accomplished)
nor can you declare it.
> (Proclus, *Commentary on Plato's Timaeus* 1.345.18; lines 3–8:
> Simplicius, *Commentary on Aristotle's Physics* 116.28; tmpc)

3. (B3) . . . for the same thing is for thinking and for being.[2]
> (Clement, *Miscellanies* 6.23; Plotinus, *Enneads* 5.1.8)

4. (B4) But gaze upon things which although absent are securely
    present to the mind.
For you will not cut off what-is from clinging to what-is,
neither being scattered everywhere in every way in order
nor being brought together.
> (Clement, *Miscellanies* 5.15)

5. (B5) . . . For me, it is indifferent
from where I am to begin: for that is where I will arrive back
    again.
> (Proclus, *Commentary on Plato's Parmenides* 1.708)

6. (B6) It is right both to say and to think that it is what-is: for
    it can be,
but nothing is not: these things I bid you to ponder.
For I < [3] > you from this first route of inquiry,
and then from that, on which mortals, knowing nothing,
wander, two-headed: for helplessness in their   5

2. Translator's note: Alternative translations: "for the same thing both can be thought of and can be"; "for thinking and being are the same."

3. There is a lacuna (gap) in all the manuscripts at this point. Diels supplied *eirgō*, so the line would be translated "I hold you back." (This would imply that there are three routes.) Two recent suggestions from scholars supply forms of the verb *archein*, "to begin," so the goddess says either "I begin for you," or "You will begin." (This implies two routes.)

breasts steers their wandering mind. They are borne along
deaf and blind alike, dazed, hordes without judgment
for whom to be and not to be are thought to be the same
and not the same, and the path of all is backward-turning.

(Simplicius, Commentary on Aristotle's
Physics 86.27–28; 117.4–13; tmpc)

7. (B7) For in no way may this prevail, that things that are
  not are;
but you, hold your thought back from this route of inquiry
and do not let habit, rich in experience, compel you along
  this route
to direct an aimless eye and an echoing ear
and tongue, but judge by reasoning (*logos*) the much-
  contested   5
examination spoken by me.

(lines 1–2: Plato, Sophist 242a; lines 2–6: Sextus
Empiricus, Against the Mathematicians 7.114; tmpc)

8. (B8) . . . Just one story of a route
is still left: that it is. On this [route] there are signs
very many, that what-is is ungenerated and imperishable,
a whole of a single kind, unshaken, and complete.
Nor was it ever, nor will it be, since it is now, all together   5
one, holding together: For what birth will you seek out for it?
How and from what did it grow? From what-is-not I will
  allow
you neither to say nor to think: For it is not to be said or
  thought
that it is not. What need would have roused it,
later or earlier, having begun from nothing, to grow?   10
In this way it is right either fully to be or not.
Nor will the force of true conviction ever permit anything
  to come to be
beside it from what-is-not. For this reason neither coming
  to be
nor perishing did Justice allow, loosening her shackles,
but she [Justice] holds it fast. And the decision about these
  things is in this: 15
is or is not; and it has been decided, as is necessary,

to leave the one [route] unthought of and unnamed (for it is
    not a true
route), so that the other [route] is and is genuine.
But how can what-is be hereafter? How can it come to be?
For if it came to be, it is not, not even if it is sometime going
    to be.   20
Thus coming-to-be has been extinguished and perishing
    cannot be investigated.
Nor is it divisible, since it is all alike,
and not at all more in any way, which would keep it from
    holding together,
or at all less, but it is all full of what-is.
Therefore it is all holding together; for what-is draws near
    to what-is.   25
But unchanging in the limits of great bonds
it is without starting or ceasing, since coming-to-be and
    perishing
have wandered very far away; and true trust drove them
    away.
Remaining the same and in the same and by itself it lies
and so remains there fixed; for mighty Necessity   30
holds it in bonds of a limit which holds it in on all sides.
For this reason it is right for what-is to be not incomplete;
for it is not lacking; otherwise, what-is would be in want of
    everything.
What is for thinking is the same as that on account of which
    there is thought.
For not without what-is, on which it depends, having been·
    solemnly pronounced,   35
will you find thinking; for nothing else either is or will be
except what-is, since precisely this is what Fate shackled
to be whole and changeless. Therefore it has been named all
    things
that mortals, persuaded that they are true, have posited
both to come to be and to perish, to be and not,   40
and to change place and alter bright color.
But since the limit is ultimate, it [namely, what-is] is
    complete
from all directions like the bulk of a ball well-rounded from
    all sides

equally matched in every way from the middle; for it is
    right
for it to be not in any way greater or lesser than in another.   45
For neither is there what-is-not—which would stop it from
    reaching
the same—nor is there any way in which what-is would be
    more than what-is in one way
and in another way less, since it is all inviolable;
for equal to itself from all directions, it meets uniformly
    with its limits.
At this point, I end for you my reliable account and thought   50
about truth. From here on, learn mortal opinions,
listening to the deceitful order of my words.
For they established two forms to name in their judgments,[4]
of which it is not right to name one—in this they have gone
    astray—
and they distinguished things opposite in body, and
    established signs   55
apart from one another—for one, the aetherial fire of flame,
mild, very light, the same as itself in every direction,
but not the same as the other; but that other one, in itself
is opposite—dark night, a dense and heavy body.
I declare to you all the ordering as it appears,   60
so that no mortal judgment may ever overtake you.
                    (Simplicius, *Commentary on Aristotle's Physics* 145.1–
                        146.25 [lines 1–52]; 39.1–9 [lines 50–61]; tmpc)

9. (B9) But since all things have been named light and night
    and the things which accord with their powers have been
        assigned to these things and those,
    all is full of light and obscure night together,
    of both equally, since neither has any share of nothing.
                    (Simplicius, *Commentary on Aristotle's Physics* 180.9–12)

10. (B10) You shall know the nature of the Aithēr and all the
    signs in the Aithēr

---

4. Translator's note: Other manuscripts give a different form of the word rendered "judgment" that requires another translation: "established judgments" (i.e., decided).

and the destructive deeds of the shining sun's pure
torch and whence they came to be,
and you shall learn the wandering deeds of the round-faced
    moon
and its nature, and you shall know also the surrounding
    heaven,   5
from what it grew and how Necessity led and shackled it
to hold the limits of the stars.
                            (Clement, *Miscellanies* 5.14; 138.1)

11. (B11) . . . how earth and sun and moon
and the Aithēr that is common to all and the Milky Way and
furthest Olympus and the hot force of the stars surged forth
to come to be.
    (Simplicius, *Commentary on Aristotle's On the Heavens* 559.22–25)

12. (B12) For the narrower <wreaths> were filled with unmixed
    fire,
the ones next to them with night, but a due amount of fire is
    inserted among it,
and in the middle of these is the goddess who governs all
    things.
For she rules over hateful birth and union of all things,
sending the female to unite with male and in opposite
    fashion,   5
male to female.
                    (Simplicius, *Commentary on Aristotle's Physics*
                    39.14–16 [lines 1–3], 31.13–17 [lines 2–6])

13. (B13) First of all gods she contrived Love.
                    (Simplicius, *Commentary on Aristotle's Physics* 39.18)

14. (B14) Night-shining foreign light wandering around earth.
                            (Plutarch, *Against Colotes* 1116A)

15. (B15) Always looking toward the rays of the sun.
                        (Plutarch, *On the Face in the Moon* 929A)

16. (B16) As on each occasion there is a mixture of the much-
    wandering limbs,

so is mind present to humans; for the same thing
is what the nature of the limbs thinks in men,
both in all and in each; for the more is thought.

(Theophrastus, *On the Senses* 3; tpc)

17. (B17) [That the male is conceived in the right part of the uterus
    has been said by others of the ancients. For Parmenides says:]
    <The goddess brought> boys <into being> on the right <side of
    the uterus>, girls on the left.

(Galen, C*ommentary on Book VI of Hippocrates' Epidemics II* 46)

18. (B18) As soon as woman and man mingle the seeds of love
    <that come from> their veins, a formative power fashions
        well-constructed bodies
    from their two differing bloods, if it maintains a balance.
    For if when the seed is mingled the powers clash
    and do not create a single <power> in the body resulting from
        the mixture,
    with double seed they will dreadfully disturb the nascent sex
        <of the child>.

(Caelius Aurelianus, *On Chronic Diseases* VI.9)

19. (B19) In this way, according to opinion (*doxa*), these things have
    grown and now are
    and afterwards after growing up will come to an end.
    And upon them humans have established a name to mark each
    one.

(Simplicius, *Commentary on Aristotle's On the Heavens* 558.9–11)

Suggestions for Further Reading

All of these entries have further bibliographies. Complete bibliographical information for collections may be found in the bibliography in
the Introduction, pp. 10–12. See also the relevant chapters in Barnes;
Guthrie; McKirahan; and Kirk, Raven, and Schofield.

Barnes, J. 1979. "Parmenides and the Eleatic One." *Archiv für Geschichte der Philosophie* 61: pp. 1–21.

Cordero, N.-L. 2004. *By Being, It Is: The Thesis of Parmenides.* Las Vegas: Parmenides Publishing.

Coxon, A. H. 2009. *The Fragments of Parmenides,* 2nd edition, revised and expanded; edited by R. D. McKirahan. Las Vegas: Parmenides Publishing.

Curd, P. 2004. *The Legacy of Parmenides: Eleatic Monism and Later Presocratic Thought,* 2nd edition. Las Vegas: Parmenides Publishing.

———. "Parmenides and After: Unity and Plurality," in Gill and Pellegrin, pp. 34–55.

Furth, M. 1968. "Elements of Eleatic Ontology." *Journal of the History of Philosophy* 6: pp. 111–32.

Gallop, D. 1984. *Parmenides of Elea: Fragments.* Toronto: University of Toronto Press.

Hussey, E. "Pythagoreans and Eleatics," in Taylor, pp. 128–74.

Kahn, C. H. "Parmenides and Plato," in Caston and Graham, eds. pp. 81–93.

———. 1969. "The Thesis of Parmenides." *Review of Metaphysics* 23: pp. 700–24.

Lesher, J. H. 1984. "Parmenides' Critique of thinking: The *poludêris elenchos* of fragment 7." *Oxford Studies in Ancient Philosophy* 2: pp. 1–30.

Long, A. A. 1963. "The Principles of Parmenides' Cosmogony." *Phronesis* 8: pp. 90–107.

McKirahan, R. "Signs and Arguments in Parmenides B8," in Curd and Graham, pp. 189–229.

Mourelatos, A. P. D. 2008. *The Route of Parmenides,* 2nd edition. Las Vegas: Parmenides Publishing.

———. 1979. "Some alternatives in interpreting Parmenides." *The Monist* 62: pp. 3–14.

Nehamas, A. 1999. "On Parmenides' three ways of inquiry." In *Virtues of Authenticity,* edited by A. Nehamas, pp. 125–37. Princeton: Princeton University Press.

———. 2002. "Parmenidean Being/Heraclitean Fire," in Caston and Graham, pp. 45–64.

Owen, G. E. L. 1960. "Eleatic Questions," in Allen and Furley, pp. 48–81.

Palmer, J. A. 2004. "Melissus and Parmenides." *Oxford Studies in Ancient Philosophy* 26: pp. 19–54.

———. 2008. "Parmenides." In *The Stanford Encyclopedia of Philosophy (Fall 2008 Edition),* edited by Edward N. Zalta. http://plato.stanford.edu/archives/fall2008/entries/parmenides/.

———. 2009. *Parmenides and Presocratic Philosophy.* Oxford: Oxford University Press.

Robinson, T. M. 1979. "Parmenides on the Real in Its Totality." *The Monist* 62: pp. 54–60.

Sedley, D. "Parmenides and Melissus," in Long, pp. 113–33.

Tarán, L. 1965. *Parmenides: A Text with Translation, Commentary, and Critical Essays.* Princeton: Princeton University Press.

Vlastos, G. 1946. "Parmenides' Theory of Knowledge." *Transactions of the American Philological Association,* 77: pp. 66–77; reprinted in Vlastos, *Studies in Greek Philosophy Vol. I: The Presocratics,* edited by D. W. Graham, pp. 153–63. Princeton: Princeton University Press.

7. ZENO OF ELEA

Almost everything we think we know about the life of Zeno of Elea comes from Plato's dialogue Parmenides. *According to Plato, Zeno was about twenty-five years younger than Parmenides and was reported to have been his lover as well as his philosophical associate. If Plato's claims are accepted, Zeno was born around 490 BCE, and he and Parmenides visited Athens in about 450 when Socrates was a young man. (It is quite unlikely that the conversation Plato reports took place, but the chronological information from Plato may be based on fact.) The only other biographical claims about Zeno come from Diogenes Laertius' not entirely reliable* Lives of the Philosophers *(9.25–9); according to Diogenes Laertius, Zeno bravely resisted a political tyranny and, despite being tortured, did not betray his comrades. Zeno explores the consequences of Parmenides' claims about what-is: in his ingenious arguments he purports to show that neither plurality nor motion is compatible with Parmenides' requirements for reality. Zeno challenges the seemingly incontrovertible evidence of our senses, and his arguments have worried and fascinated philosophers from ancient times to the present.*

1. (29A11, A12) Once Parmenides and Zeno came to Athens for the Great Panathenaic festival. Parmenides was quite an elderly man, very gray, but fine and noble in appearance, just about sixty-five years old. Zeno was then almost forty, of a good height and handsome to see. The story goes that he had been Parmenides' young lover. . . . Socrates and many others <were> eager to listen to Zeno's treatise, for he had then brought it to Athens for the first time. Socrates was then very young. Zeno himself read it to them. . . . When Socrates had heard it, he asked Zeno to read again the first hypothesis of the first argument. When he had read it, he said, "How do you mean this, Zeno? If things that are are many, they must therefore be both like and unlike, but this is impossible.

For unlike things cannot be like, nor can like things be unlike. Isn't that what you are saying?"

—*Zeno:* Yes.

—*Socrates:* Now if it is impossible for unlike things to be like and for like things to be unlike, is it also impossible for things to be many? For if they were many they would have impossible attributes. Is this the point of your arguments—to contend, against all that is said, that things are not many? And do you think that each of your arguments proves this?

—*Zeno:* You have well understood the purpose of the whole work.

—*Socrates:* I understand, Parmenides, that Zeno here wants to be identified with you by his treatise as well as his friendship, for he has written somewhat in the same style as you, but by changing it he is trying to make us think he is saying something else. For in your poem you declare that the all is one and you do a good job of proving this, while he declares that it is not many, and furnishes many impressive proofs. Now when one of you says it is one and the other that it is not many, and each speaks so as to seem not to have said any of the same things, though you are saying practically the same things, what you have said appears beyond the rest of us.

—*Zeno:* Yes, Socrates, but you have not completely understood the truth of the treatise. . . . It is actually a defense of Parmenides' argument against those who try to make fun of it, saying that if what-is is one, the argument has many ridiculous consequences which contradict it. Now my treatise opposes the advocates of plurality and pays them back the same and more, aiming to prove that their hypothesis, "if there are many things," suffers still more ridiculous consequences than the hypothesis that there is one, if anyone follows it through sufficiently. I wrote it in this spirit of competitiveness when I was young, and then someone stole it, so I did not even have the chance to consider whether it should be made public.

(Plato, *Parmenides* 127b–128d)

2. (A16) Zeno stated that if anyone could make clear to him what the one is, he would be able to speak of the things that are.

(Eudemus, *Physics* fr. 7, quoted in Simplicius, *Commentary on Aristotle's Physics* 97.12–13)

3. (B2) For if it should be added to something else that exists, it would not make it any larger. For if it were of no size and were added, nothing it is added to could increase in size. And so it follows immediately that what is added is nothing. But if the other thing is no smaller when it is subtracted and it is not increased when it is added, clearly the thing added or subtracted is nothing.

   (Simplicius, *Commentary on Aristotle's Physics* 139.11–15)

4. (B1) If it is, each thing must have some size and thickness, and part of it must be apart from the rest. And the same reasoning holds concerning the part that is in front. For that too will have size, and part of it will be in front. Now to say this once is the same thing as to keep saying it forever. For no such part of it will be the last or unrelated to another. Therefore if there are many things, they must be both small and large; so small as not to have size, but so large as to be infinite.

   (Simplicius, *Commentary on Aristotle's Physics* 141.2–8)

5. (B3) If there are many, they must be just as many as they are, nei-ther more nor less. But if they are as many as they are, they must be limited. If there are many things, the things that are are unlimited, since between things that are there are always others, and still oth-ers between those. Therefore the things that are are unlimited.

   (Simplicius, *Commentary on Aristotle's Physics* 140.29–33)

6. (A25) There are four of Zeno's arguments about motion that present difficulties for those who try to solve them. First is the argument that says that there is no motion because that which is moving must reach the midpoint before the end. . . . It is always necessary to traverse half the distance, but these are infinite, and it is impos-sible to get through things that are infinite. . . .

   (Aristotle, *Physics* 6.9 239b9–13; *Physics* 8.8 263a5–6)

7. (A26) The second <argument> is the one called the Achilles. This is to the effect that the slowest as it runs will never be caught by the quickest. For the pursuer must first reach the point from which the pursued departed, so that the slower must always be some

distance in front. This is the same argument as the Dichotomy,[1] but it differs in not dividing the given magnitude in half.

(Aristotle, *Physics* 6.9 239b14–20)

8. (A25) For this reason Zeno's argument falsely assumes that it is impossible to traverse or come into contact with an infinite number of things individually in a finite time. For both length and time and generally everything that is continuous are called infinite in two ways: infinite in division and infinite with respect to their extremities. Now it is impossible to come into contact with things infinite in quantity in a finite time, but it is possible to do so with things that are infinite in division. For time itself too is infinite in this way. And so, it follows that it traverses the infinite in an infinite and not a finite time, and comes into contact with infinite things in infinite, not finite times.

(Aristotle, *Physics* 6.2 233a21–31)

9. This solution is sufficient to use against the person who raised the question (for he asked whether it is possible to traverse or count infinite things in a finite time), but insufficient for the facts of the matter and the truth.

(Aristotle, *Physics* 8.8 263a15–18; not in DK)

10. (A27) Zeno makes a mistake in reasoning. For if, he says, everything is always at rest when it occupies a space equal to itself, and what is moving is always "at a now," the moving arrow is motionless.

(Aristotle, *Physics* 6.9 239b5–7)

The third argument is the one just stated, that the arrow is stopped while it is moving. This follows from assuming that time is composed of "nows." If this is not conceded, the deduction will not go through.

(Aristotle, *Physics* 6.9 239b30–33)

11. (A28) The fourth argument is about equal bodies moving in a stadium alongside equal bodies in the opposite direction, the one

---

1. The Dichotomy is Aristotle's name for Zeno's first argument (A25, no. 6 above).

group moving from the end of the stadium, the other from the middle, at equal speed. He claims in this argument that it follows that half the time is equal to the double. The mistake is in thinking that an equal magnitude moving with equal speed takes an equal time in passing something moving as it does in passing something at rest. But this is false. Let *A*'s represent the equal stationary bodies, *B*'s the bodies beginning from the middle, equal in number and size to the *A*'s, and *C*'s the bodies beginning from the end, equal in number and size to these and having the same speed as the *B*'s. It follows that the first *B* is at the end at the same time as the first *C*, as the *B*'s and *C*'s move alongside one another, and the first *C* has completed the process of coming alongside all the *B*'s, but the first *B* has completed the process of coming alongside half the *A*'s. And so the time is half. For each of them is alongside each thing for an equal time. It follows simultaneously that the first *B* has moved alongside all the *C*'s, for the first *C* and the first *B* will be at the opposite ends simultaneously, because both have been alongside the *A*'s for an equal amount of time.

(Aristotle, *Physics* 6.9 239b33–240a17)

12.[2] (A24) If place exists, where is it? For everything that exists is in a place. Therefore if place exists, then place is in a place. This goes on to infinity. Therefore, place does not exist.

(Simplicius, *Commentary on Aristotle's Physics* 562.3–6; Aristotle, *Physics* 4.3 210b22–23, 4.1 209a23–25; Eudemus, *Physics* fr. 42, quoted by Simplicius, *Commentary on Aristotle's Physics* 563.25–28)

13.[3] (A29) —*Zeno:* Tell me, Protagoras, does a single millet seed make a noise when it falls, or one ten-thousandth of a millet seed?
—*Protagoras:* No.
—*Zeno:* Does a bushel of millet seeds make a noise when it falls, or doesn't it?
—*Protagoras:* It does.

2. Translator's note: This argument is reported variously; what follows is the gist of the argument.

3. Translator's note: This argument is preserved in a "theatrical version," a dialogue between Zeno and the Sophist Protagoras, which is probably not the way it originally appeared.

—*Zeno:* But isn't there a ratio between the bushel of millet seeds and one millet seed, or one ten-thousandth of a millet seed?

—*Protagoras:* Yes there is.

—*Zeno:* So won't there be the same ratios of their sounds to one another? For as the things that make the noise <are to one another>, so are the noises <to one another>. But since this is so, if the bushel of millet seeds makes a noise, so will a single millet seed and one ten-thousandth of a millet seed.

(Simplicius, *Commentary on Aristotle's Physics* 1108.18–25)

13a. (Response from Aristotle) It does not follow that if a given motive power causes a certain amount of motion, half that power will cause motion either of any particular amount or in any length of time: otherwise, one man might move a ship, if the power of the ship-haulers is divided into their number and the distance that all of them move it.

(Aristotle, *Physics* 7.5 250a16–19; not in DK)

Suggestions for Further Reading

All of these entries have further bibliographies. Complete bibliographical information for collections may be found in the bibliography in the Introduction, pp. 10–12. See also the relevant chapters in Barnes; Guthrie; McKirahan; and Kirk, Raven, and Schofield.

Curd, P. K. 1993. "Eleatic monism in Zeno and Melissus." *Ancient Philosophy* 13: pp. 1–22.

Glazebrook, T. 2001. "Zeno against mathematical physics." *Journal of the History of Ideas* 62: pp. 193–210.

Grünbaum, A. 1968. *Modern Science and Zeno's Paradoxes.* London: Allen and Unwin.

Huggett, N., ed. 1999. *Space from Zeno to Einstein: Classic Readings with a Contemporary Commentary.* Cambridge, MA: MIT Press.

———. 2008. "Zeno's Paradoxes." In *The Stanford Encyclopedia of Philosophy (Fall 2008 Edition),* edited by Edward N. Zalta. http://plato.stanford.edu/archives/fall2008/entries/paradox-zeno/.

Knorr, W. 1983. "Zeno's Paradoxes Still in Motion." *Ancient Philosophy* 3: pp. 55–66.

Lear, J. 1981. "A Note on Zeno's Arrow." *Phronesis* 26: pp. 91–104.

Lee, H. D. P. 1936, 1967. *Zeno of Elea: A Text with Translation and Notes*. Cambridge: Cambridge University Press. Repr. Amsterdam: Hakkert.

Lewis, E. 1999. "The Dogmas of Indivisibility: On the Origins of Ancient Atomism." *Proceedings of the Boston Area Colloquium in Ancient Philosophy* 15: pp. 1–21.

Makin, S. 1998. "Zeno of Elea." In *Routledge Encyclopedia of Philosophy*, vol. 9, edited by E. Craig, pp. 843–53. London and New York: Routledge.

———. 1982. "Zeno on Plurality." *Phronesis* 27: pp. 223–38.

Matson, W. I. 2001. "Zeno Moves!" In *Essays in Ancient Greek Philosophy VI: Before Plato*, edited by A. Preus, pp. 87–108. Albany: SUNY Press.

McKirahan, R. D. 1999. "Zeno." In *The Cambridge Companion to Early Greek Philosophy*, edited by A. A. Long, pp. 134–58. Cambridge: Cambridge University Press.

Owen, G. E. L. 1958. "Zeno and the mathematicians." *Proceedings of the Aristotelian Society* 58: pp. 199–222.

Palmer, John. 2008. "Zeno of Elea." In *The Stanford Encyclopedia of Philosophy (Fall 2008 Edition)*, edited by Edward N. Zalta. http://plato.stanford.edu/archives/fall2008/entries/zeno-elea/.

Russell, B. 1914. "The Problem of Infinity Considered Historically." In his *Our Knowledge of the External World*, pp. 159–88. London: Open Court.

Salmon, W. C., ed. 2001. *Zeno's Paradoxes*. Indianapolis: Hackett.

Vlastos, G. 1967, 1993. "Zeno of Elea." In *The Encyclopedia of Philosophy*, vol. 8, edited by P. Edwards, pp. 369–79. New York and London: Macmillan. Reprinted in Vlastos, *Studies in Greek Philosophy, vol. 1: The Presocratics*, edited by D. W. Graham, pp. 241–63. Princeton: Princeton University Press.

8. EMPEDOCLES
OF ACRAGAS

Born in Acragas, in Sicily, around 492 BCE, Empedocles belongs to the generation of Presocratics who come after Parmenides. He is known to have visited the southern Italian mainland, and while his work shows his familiarity with Parmenides, there are also signs of the influence of Pythagoreanism, the other great southern Italian philosophical movement. At home in Acragas, he seems to have been an active politician, supporting democracy against oligarchy, even though his own aristocratic family connections might have made that support unexpected. Empedocles was a philosopher, a medical man, and a truly flamboyant figure. According to ancient reports, he dressed ostentatiously (there are stories of rich purple robes, a golden diadem, and bronze sandals), he claimed remarkable powers for himself, and in fragment B112 (no. 1 below) he says of himself, "I go about among you, an immortal god, no longer mortal, / honored among all, as it seems, / wreathed with headbands and blooming garlands." There are many stories of his fantastic activities: reportedly a woman with no pulse who had stopped breathing was kept alive by him for a month; he diverted two streams in the city of Selinus (on the south coast of Sicily) in order to rid the city of a plague (and was said to have been honored as a god as a result). Empedocles was exiled from his home and was said to have died in the Peloponnese, although, given his character, it is not surprising that more exciting tales were told about his death. Diogenes Laertius reports that Empedocles, desiring to demonstrate that he was indeed a god, leapt into the crater of Mount Aetna.

Although these stories suggest a flashy and eccentric figure, we should not lose sight of the fact that Empedocles constructed a serious and complicated theory of the cosmos and the place of human beings in it. Like Parmenides, he wrote in verse; his subjects included both natural philosophy (physics and the development of the cosmos) and inquiry into how human beings ought to live (ethical and religious topics). For a long time scholars debated how, if at all, these two main areas of interest were related. New study, and the discovery of some new texts, now show without a doubt that Empedocles regarded these questions as connected, and that the material from the two was thoroughly integrated. There remains the question of how many different works

Empedocles composed; traditionally there have been thought to be at least two separate poems, usually called Physics *and* Purifications. *Although we now know that the physical and purificatory material were not viewed by Empedocles as entirely distinct, the question of how many poems Empedocles wrote remains open.*

Empedocles claimed that the numerous basic realities of the cosmos are entities with the features of basic reality for which Parmenides had argued. Although these basic entities are eternally real and unchanging in their natures, their mixture and separation cause the world of the senses. Empedocles says that there are six such basic things in the cosmos, each a genuine being in the Parmenidean sense: the roots (as Empedocles refers to them) Earth, Water, Air, and Fire (later called "elements" by Aristotle), and two forces, Love and Strife. The roots are mixed and separated (by Love and Strife) to produce the world that we sense and are a part of; this mixture and separation take the place of coming-to-be and passing-away, since the ingredients remain all through the changes. In selections 87 (B96) and 88 (B98) Empedocles provides "recipes" for such phenomenal things as bone and blood. At the same time, under the waxing and waning of the comparative strengths of the forces of Love and Strife the cosmos undergoes cycles from complete mixture of the roots to their complete separation: how many cycles there are, and the events within those cycles are subjects of controversy among commentators. Within the cycles, living things come to be and pass away; Empedocles' system includes daimones *(singular,* daimōn*) which are divinities of some sort. These* daimones *undergo many lives, apparently because of some transgression. Although they, like the gods, are called "long-lived" by Empedocles, they are not immortal, for they, like the roots of which they are made, are all absorbed into the complete mixture of the roots at the height of Love's power. Only the roots and Love and Strife are genuinely immortal, subject neither to coming-to-be or passing-away. The destiny of the* daimones *is connected with the sorts of lives they lead, and it is in the nature, behavior, and fates of the* daimones *that Empedocles' natural and religious views come together.*

Note on the text and the order of the fragments: In the 1990s scholars discovered that previously unexamined papyrus fragments contained some seventy-four lines of poetry (in varying states of completeness). Because the papyrus contained previously known lines as well as new, previously unknown material, the editors were able to identify the author as Empedocles. The Strasbourg Papyrus (so named because it has been in the collections of the Strasbourg library since the early part of the twentieth century), reconstructed and translated, provided important new material for Empedocles studies, and that material is included here. The ordering of the fragments of Empedocles is controversial; scholars have strong views and serious disagreements about the proper order. Here, the order is that of the translator, Richard McKirahan.[1]

1. (31B112) Friends who dwell in the great city on the yellow
      Acragas
   on the heights of the citadel, you whose care is good deeds,
   respectful havens for strangers, untouched by evil,
   hail! I go about among you, an immortal god, no longer
      mortal,
   honored among all, as it seems,   5
   wreathed with headbands and blooming garlands.
   Wherever I go to their flourishing cities,
   I am revered by all—men and women. And they follow
      together
   in tens of thousands, inquiring where lies the path to profit,
   some in need of prophecy, while others,   10
   pierced for a long time with harsh pains,
   asked to hear the voice of healing for all diseases.
                  (Diogenes Laertius, *Lives of the Philosophers* 8.61–2 [lines
                         1–10]; Clement, *Miscellanies* 6.30 [lines 9–11])

2. (B114) Friends, I know that truth is in the words
   I will speak. But very difficult
   for men and spiteful is the invasion of conviction into their
      minds.
                                        (Clement, *Miscellanies* 5.9)

3. (B113) But why do I insist on these matters as if I were
      accomplishing something great,
   if I am superior to mortal humans who perish many times?
                  (Sextus Empiricus, *Against the Mathematicians* 1.302)

---

1. There are a few exceptions and omissions in the texts given here. For a discussion of McKirahan's ordering principles, see his *Philosophy Before Socrates*, 2nd edition, p. 230 n. 1.

4. (B128) Nor was there any god Ares among them nor
     Kudoimos ["battle-din"]
   nor King Zeus, nor Kronos nor Poseidon,
   but there was Queen Cypris. . . .
   Her they propitiated with reverent statues
   and painted figures and unguents with varied odors,   5
   and with offerings of unmixed myrrh and fragrant
     frankincense,
   pouring on the ground libations of yellow honey.
   No altar was drenched with the unspeakable slaughter of
     bulls,
   but this was the greatest abomination among humans,   10
   to tear out life and devour the noble limbs.
               (Porphyry, *On Abstinence* 2.20 [lines 1–8]; 2.27 [lines 8–11])

5. (B130) All were tame and kindly toward humans—
   both animals and birds—and friendliness burned brightly.
            (Scholium in Nicander, *Antidotes against Poisonous Bites* 453)

6. (B78) [Empedocles declares that evergreens and continuously
     fruiting trees flourish] with bounties of fruits in the air each
     year.
                 (Theophrastus, *On Plants: The Explanations* 1.13.2)

7. (B132) Blessed is he who possesses wealth of divine intelligence
   but wretched is he whose concern is a dim opinion about the gods.
                              (Clement, *Miscellanies* 5.140)

8. (B115) There is an oracle of Necessity, an ancient decree of
     the gods,
   eternal and sealed with broad oaths,
   that whenever anyone pollutes his own dear limbs with the
     sin of bloodshed,
   . . .[2] commits offense and swears a false oath
   —divinities (*daimones*) who possess immensely long life   5
   he wanders away from the blessed ones for thrice ten
     thousand seasons,

---

2. The first part of the line is missing, so lines 4 and 5 are unclear. They probably, as McKirahan says, "elaborate 'anyone' in line 3."

through time growing to be all different kinds of mortals,
taking the difficult paths of life one after another.
For the force of Aithēr pursues them to the sea
and the sea spits them out onto the surface of the earth,
and the   10
earth into the rays
of the shining sun, and he [the sun] casts them into the
   vortices of Aithēr.
One receives them after another, but all hate them.
Of these I am now one, a fugitive from the gods and a
   wanderer,
putting my reliance on raving Strife.

> (Hippolytus, *Refutation of All Heresies* 7.29.14–23 [lines
> 1–2, 4–14]; Plutarch, *On Exile* 607C [lines 1, 3, 5–13])

9. (B142) Neither, then, the roofed halls of aegis-bearing Zeus
   nor the house of Hades <? receives> him.

> (Voll. Herc. N 1012 col 18)

10. (B125) For from living forms it [? Strife] was making dead
    ones, changing them.

> (Clement, *Miscellanies* 3.14.2)

11. (B126) Wrapping <it> in an alien garb of flesh.

> (Plutarch, *On Eating Flesh* 998c)

12. (B117) For I have already been born as a boy and a girl
    and a bush and a bird and a <mute> fish <from the sea>.[3]

> (Diogenes Laertius, *Lives of the Philosophers* 8.77)

13. (B119) From such honor and how great an amount of bliss . . .

> (Plutarch, *On Exile* 17 607D)

14. (B118) I wept and wailed upon seeing the unfamiliar place.

> (Clement, *Miscellanies* 3.14)

15. (B121) . . . Joyless place,
    where bloodshed, anger, and tribes of other spirits of death

---

3. Translator's note: The words in brackets are conjectures; the text is
corrupt.

and squalid diseases, rotting, and works of dissolution[4]
wander in darkness through the meadow of disaster (*atē*).
(Hierocles, *Commentary on the Golden Verses* 54.2–3;
Proclus, *Commentary on Plato's Cratylus* 97.23)

16. (B124) Alas! Wretched race of mortals! Unfortunate!
Out of such quarreling and groaning were you born.
(Clement, *Miscellanies* 3.14)

17. (B136) Will you not cease from harsh-sounding bloodshed?
Do you not see
that you are devouring each other in the carelessness of your
thought?
(Sextus Empiricus, *Against the Mathematicians* 9.119)

18. (B138) Having drawn off life [*psychē*] with bronze.
(Aristotle, *Poetics* 1457b13)

19. (B137) A father lifts up his own dear son who has changed
form,
and, praying, slaughters him, committing a great folly. And
they are at a loss,
sacrificing him as he entreats them. But he, refusing to hear
the cries,
slaughters him and attends an evil feast in his halls.
Likewise a son seizes his father and children their mother,   5
and tearing out their life, devour the dear flesh.
(Sextus Empiricus, *Against the Mathematicians* 9.129)

20. (B145) Therefore, distraught with harsh evils,
you will never relieve your spirit from wretched distress.
(Clement, *Protrepticus* 2.27.3)

21. (B135) But what is lawful for all extends far through the wide-
ruling
Aithēr and through the immense glare.
(Aristotle, *Rhetoric* 1.13 1373b6–17)

4. Translator's note: This line may not belong here.

22. (B144) Fast from evil.

> (Plutarch, *The Control of Anger* 464B)

23. (B140) Keep completely away from laurel leaves!

> (Plutarch, *Table Talk* 646d)

24. (B141) Wretched, wholly wretched! Keep your hands off beans!

> (Aulus Gellius, *Athenian Nights* 4.11.1–2 and 4.11.9–10)

25. (B127) Among beasts they come into being as lions whose lairs
  are in the mountains
and their beds on the ground, and as laurels among shaggy
  trees.

> (Aelian, *Natural History* 12.7)

26. (B146) In the end they are prophets and bards and physicians
and chiefs among men on earth,
and from there they arise as gods mightiest in honors.

> (Clement, *Miscellanies* 4.150)

27. (B147) Sharing the same hearth and table with other immortals
relieved of manly distress, unwearied.

> (Clement, *Miscellanies* 5.122)

28. (B133) It is not possible to reach and approach <the divine> with
  our eyes
or grasp it with our hands, by which the most powerful
highway of persuasion strikes the minds of men.

> (Clement, *Miscellanies* 5.81)

29. (B131) For if, immortal Muse, for the sake of any ephemeral
  creature
it pleased you that our concerns should come to your thoughts,
be present once again to me, Kalliopeia, now as I pray,
as I reveal a good account about the blessed gods.

> (Hippolytus, *Refutation of All Heresies* 7.31.3)

30. (B1) But you listen, Pausanias, son of wise-minded Anchites.

> (Diogenes Laertius, *Lives of the Philosophers* 8.60)

31. (B111) You will learn all the drugs there are as a safeguard
　　　against evils and old age,
　　since for you alone shall I bring to pass all these things.
　　You will stop the force of the tireless winds that rush
　　over the earth and devastate the plowed fields with their
　　　blasts.
　　And, if you wish, you will arouse their breath again.　　　　　5
　　You will change black rain into seasonable dryness
　　for people, and summer drought you will change
　　into tree-nourishing waters that dwell in the sky.
　　And you will bring back from Hades the strength of a
　　　dead man.
　　　　　　　　(Diogenes Laertius, *Lives of the Philosophers* 8.59)

32. (B5) [Empedocles advised Pausanias] to cover up [his teachings]
　　　within a voiceless heart (*phrēn*).
　　　　　　　　　　　　　　(Plutarch, *Table Talk* 728E)

33. (B4) It is highly typical of evil people to mistrust what prevails;
　　but learn how the trustworthy reports from our Muse command,
　　by splitting apart the account (*logos*) in your entrails.
　　　　　　　　　　　　　(Clement, *Miscellanies* 5.18.4)

34. (B2) Narrow are the means of apprehension spread
　　　throughout the limbs.
　　Many wretched things burst in which blunt the thoughts.
　　People see a tiny part of life during their time
　　and swift-fated they are taken away and fly like smoke,
　　persuaded only of whatever each of them has chanced to
　　　meet　　　　　　　　　　　　　　　　　　　　　5
　　as they were driven everywhere; but everyone boasts that
　　　he discovered the whole.
　　These things are not in this way to be seen or heard by men
　　or grasped with the mind. But you, since you have turned
　　　aside to this place,
　　will learn; mortal cunning has reached no further.
　　　　　　　　(Sextus Empiricus, *Against the Mathematicians* 7.123)

35.[5] (B3b) Nor will it compel you to take away the blossoms of
    fair-famed honor from mortals
on the condition that you say in rashness more than is
    holy—
and <only> then sit upon the summits of wisdom.
But come, look with every means of apprehension, in
    whatever way each thing is clear,
not holding any sight more in trust than <what comes>
    through hearing,   5
or loud-sounding hearing above the things made clear by
    the tongue,
and do not at all hold back trust in any of the other limbs,
wherever there is a channel for understanding, but
understand each thing in whatever way it is clear.
                         (Sextus Empiricus, *Against the Mathematicians* 7.125)

36. (B3a) But, gods, avert their madness from my tongue,
and lead a pure stream from holy mouths.
And you, much-remembering maiden Muse with white arms,
I entreat—bring the things it is right for creatures of a day
to hear, driving your easily-steered chariot from the halls of
    reverence.
                         (Sextus Empiricus, *Against the Mathematicians* 7.123)

37. (B6) Hear first the four roots of all things:
shining Zeus and life-bringing Hera and Aidoneus
and Nestis, who with her tears gives moisture to the source of
    mortals.
                                                          (Aëtius 1.3.20)

38. (B7) Ungenerated.
                         (Hesychius, *Lexicon* s.v. *agennēta* [Empedocles
                              used this word to describe the elements])

39. (B8) I will tell you another thing. There is coming-to-be of not
    a single one of all

---

5. Translator's note: DK fr. 3 is divided into two parts, since it is implausible to
identify the addressee of fragment 35 as the Muse who is addressed in fragment 36 line 3.

mortal things, nor is there any end of destructive death,
but only mixture, and separation of what is mixed,
and nature (*phusis*) is the name given to them by humans.
(Plutarch, *Against Colotes* 1111F–12A)

40. (B11) Fools. For their thoughts are not far-reaching—
those who expect that there comes to be what previously was
   not,
or that anything perishes and is completely destroyed.
(Plutarch, *Against Colotes* 1113C)

41. (B9) Whenever they arrive in the Aithēr mixed so as to form
   a man
or one of the wild beasts or bushes
or birds, that is when <people> speak of coming into being;
and whenever they are separated, that <is what they call>
   the ill-starred fate of death.
They do not call it as is right, but I myself too assent to their
   convention.   5
(Plutarch, *Against Colotes* 1113D)

42. (B15) A man who is wise in his thoughts (*phrēn*) would not
   divine such things as this—
that as long as they live what they in fact call life
they are, and have things wretched and good,
but before they took on the fixed form of mortals and after they
   have
dissolved, they are then nothing.
(Plutarch, *Against Colotes* 1113D)

43. (B12) For it is impossible to come to be from what in no way is,
and it is not to be accomplished and is unheard of that what is
   perishes absolutely.
For it will always be where a person thrusts it each time.
([Aristotle], *Melissus, Xenophanes, Gorgias* 2 975b1–4)

44. (B13) None of the whole is either empty or overfull.
(Aëtius 1.18.2)

45. (B14) Of the whole, nothing is empty; from where, then, could
  anything come to be added to it?

  ([Aristotle], *Melissus, Xenophanes, Gorgias* 2 976b23)

46. (B16) For they are as they were previously and will be, and
  never, I think,

  will endless time be empty of both of these.

  (Hippolytus, *Refutation of All Heresies* 7.29.9)

47. (B17 + Strasbourg Papyrus, *ensemble* a) I will tell a double
  story. For

  at one time they grew to be only one   *(232)*[6]

  out of many, but at another they grew apart to be many
    out of one.

  Double is the generation of mortal things, and double their
    decline.

  For the coming together of all things gives birth to one
    [namely,

  generation and decline] and destroys it,   *(235)*

  and the other is nurtured and flies away when they grow
    apart again.   5

  And these never cease continually interchanging,

  at one time all coming together into one by Love

  and at another each being borne apart by the hatred of
    Strife.

  Thus in that they have learned to grow to be one out of
    many   *(240)*

  and in that they again spring apart as many when the one
    grows apart,   10

  in that way they come to be, and their life is not lasting,

  but in that they never cease interchanging continually,

  in this way they are always unchanging in a cycle.

  But come, listen to my words, for learning increases
    wisdom.   *(245)*

6. Translator's note: The line numbers in parentheses are given as Empedocles'
text is reconstructed by Primavesi (2008). This numbering is based on the identification of the three hundredth line in the poem by a mark in the margin of
the last line in *ensemble a* of the Strasbourg Papyrus.

For as I previously said, while declaring the bounds of my
    words,   15
I will tell a double story. For at one time they grew to be
    only one
out of many, but at another they grew apart to be many out
    of one:
fire and water and earth and the immense height of air,
and deadly Strife apart from them, equal in all directions   *(250)*
and Love among them, equal in length and breadth.   20
Behold her with your mind, and do not sit with your eyes
    staring in amazement.
She is also recognized as innate in mortal limbs.
Through her they have kindly thoughts and do peaceful
    deeds,
calling her by the appellation Joy and also Aphrodite.   *(255)*
No mortal man has seen her spinning   25
among them. But listen to the undeceitful course of my
    account.
For these [the four elements] are all equal and of the same
    age,
but each rules in its own province and possesses its own
    individual character,
but they dominate in their turn as time revolves.   *(260)*
And nothing is added to them or subtracted,   30
for if they were perishing continuously, they would no
    longer be.
But what could increase this totality? And where would it
    come from?
And how could it perish, since nothing is empty of these?
But there are just these very things, and running through
    one another   *(265)*
at different times they come to be different things and yet
    are always and continuously the same.   35
{But under Love}[7] we come together into one *kosmos,*

7. Translator's note: At this point begins the section for which the papyrus is our
only evidence. There are numerous gaps in the preserved text, some of which
can be restored with a good degree of confidence from other Empedoclean
verses. For the rest, the choice is either to stay close to what the papyrus contains or to fill in the gaps by conjecture informed by one's knowledge of the

{whereas under Strife it [that is, the ordered whole] grew
    apart, so as} to be many from one,
from which [that is, many things] all things that were and
    are and will be in the future
have sprouted: trees and men and women,   (270)
and beasts and birds and fishes nurtured in water,   40
and long-lived gods highest in honors.
{Under her [that is, Strife]} they never cease, continually
    darting in dense whirls . . .
without pausing, and never . . .   (275)
but {many} lifetimes before . . .   45
before passing from them . . .
{and never cease} continually darting {in all directions}
for neither the sun . . .
{the onrush full of this} . . .   (280)
nor any of the others . . .   50
but interchanging in a circle {they dart in all directions}
for at that time the impassable earth runs, and the sun as
    well
{and the sphere [that is, the celestial sphere]} as large as
    even now {it is judged} by men {to be}
in the same way all these things {were running} through
    one another   (285)
{and having been driven away, each of them reached}
    different {and peculiar} places   55
{self-willed}; and we were coming together in the mid-most
    places to be only one.
But when indeed Strife passed through {and reached} the
    depths

---

author's vocabulary, style, and views. The translation provided is based on
two versions of the Greek text and the accompanying translations: the original
publication by Martin and Primavesi (1999), and the text printed in Inwood
(2001). Inwood is more conservative, staying closer to the papyrus text, while
Martin and Primavesi are more willing to propose ways to restore missing
material. The words enclosed in curly brackets translate supplements of Martin
and Primavesi that Inwood does not include. The purpose has been to offer a
readable translation while marking places where there is a good chance that
the text translated is not what Empedocles wrote.

{of the swirl,} and Love {comes to be} in the midst of the
    vortex,
{then} indeed all these things come together to be only one. *(290)*
{Strive eagerly} so that {my account may arrive} not only
    through ears,   60
{and behold} the unerring truths that are around while
    you listen to me.
I shall show you also through your eyes {where they [that
    is, the elements] find} a larger body:
first, the coming together and development {of the
    offspring} . . . and all that now still remain of this
    {generation}   *(295)*
both among the {wild species} of mountain-roaming beasts   65
and among the twofold offspring of men, {and also among}
the offspring of root-bearing {fields} and vine-mounting
    {clusters of grapes}.
From these stories bring back to your mind undeceiving
    evidence,
for you will see the coming together and development of
    the offspring.   *(300)*
        (Simplicius, *Commentary on Aristotle's Physics* 158.1–159.4
        [lines 1–35] + Strasbourg Papyrus *ensemble* a [lines 26–69])

48. (B20 + Strasbourg Papyrus, *ensemble* c)
{Where Love and Strife have} their guiding {counsels}   *(301)*
This is very clear in the mass of mortal limbs:
sometimes we come together through Love into one, all the
limbs that have obtained a body, at the peak of flourishing
    life,
while at other times, split apart through evil quarrels   *(305)* 5
they wander each kind separately on the furthest shore
    of life.
And it happens the same way for bushes and water-homed
    fishes
and mountain-dwelling beasts and wing-propelled birds.
        (Simplicius, *Commentary on Aristotle's Physics*
        1124.7–18 + Strasbourg Papyrus, *ensemble* c)

49. (B21) But come, behold this witness of my previous
    discourse,   *(309)*

if anything in the foregoing was feeble in form:
the sun, brilliant to see and hot everywhere,
all the immortal things that are drenched in the heat and
    shining light,
and rain, in all things dark and cold,   5
and from earth stream forth things rooted and solid.
In Anger they are all apart and have separate forms,   (*315*)
but they come together in Love and yearn for one another.
From these all things that were and are and will be in the
    future
have sprouted: trees and men and women,   10
and beasts and birds and fishes nurtured in water,
and long-lived gods highest in honors.   (*320*)
For there are just these things, and running through one
    another
they come to have different appearances, for mixture
    changes them.
        (Simplicius, *Commentary on Aristotle's Physics* 159.13–26)

50. (B76 + Strasbourg Papyrus, *ensemble* b)
This [i.e., fire] is found in the case of heavy-backed shells
    of sea-dwelling creatures.   (*324*)
. . .   (*325*)
There you will see earth {dwelling} in the uppermost
    parts of the flesh . . .   (*327*)
and indeed truly [in the flesh] of stony-skinned tritons and
    turtles
. . . of horned stags
. . . saying   (*330*)
        (Plutarch, *The Face in the Moon* 14 927F–928A and
      Table Talk 1.2.5 618B + Strasbourg Papyrus, *ensemble* b)

51. (B23) As when painters decorate votive offerings—
men through cunning well taught in their skill—
who when they take the many-colored pigments in their
    hands,
mixing in harmony more of these and less of those,
out of them they produce shapes similar to all things,   5
creating trees and men and women
and beasts and birds and fishes nurtured in water

and long-lived gods highest in honors.
So let not deception compel your mind (*phrēn*) to believe
    that there is from anywhere else
a source of mortal things, all the endless numbers of   10
things that have come to be manifest,
but know these things distinctly, having heard the story
    from a god.
            (Simplicius, *Commentary on Aristotle's Physics* 160.1–11)

52. (B26) They dominate in turn as the cycle evolves,
and they decrease into one another and grow in their turn,
    as destined.
For there are just these things, and running through one
    another
they come to be both humans and the tribes of other beasts,
at one time coming together into a single *kosmos* by Love   5
and at another each being borne apart again by the hatred
    of Strife,
until they grow together into one, the whole, and become
    subordinate.
Thus in that they have learned to grow to be one out of
    many
and in that they again spring apart as many when the one
    grows apart,
in that way they come to be and their life is not lasting,   10
but in that these never cease interchanging continually,
in this way they are always unchanging in a cycle.
         (Simplicius, *Commentary on Aristotle's Physics* 33.19–34.3)

53. (B139 + Strasbourg Papyrus, *ensemble* d)
. . . to fall apart from one another and encounter their fate
very much against their will, rotting through mournful
    necessity;
But for those who now have Love . . .
the Harpies will be present with the tokens {in the lottery}
    of death.
Alas that the pitiless day did not destroy me   5
before I devised with my claws wicked deeds for the sake
    of eating flesh.
{But now} in vain in this {storm} I wet my cheeks

{for we are approaching} a very deep {whirl,} I think,
{and} although they do not wish it, {tens of thousands of}
   pains will be present in their mind
{to humans,} but we will again mount {you} on {that}
   account: 10
{when} an untiring flame happened to meet
. . . bringing on a woeful mixture
. . . things that could produce offspring were born
. . . I entered the final place
. . . with a scream and a cry   15
. . . having obtained {the meadow of Disaster}
. . . around . . . earth.

> (Strasbourg Papyrus *ensemble* d + Porphyry
> *On Abstinence* 2.31 [lines 5–6])

54. (B25) For indeed it is a fine thing to tell twice what one must.

> (Scholium in Plato's *Gorgias* 498e)

55. (B22) For all these things—shining sun and earth and
   heaven
and sea—are united with their own parts,
all that are split off and have come to be in mortal things.
In the same way, all that are more fitted for mixture
are made alike by Aphrodite and have come to love one
   another.   5
But greatest enemies are those furthest separated from one
   another
in birth and mixture and molded forms,
in every way unaccustomed to be together and very mournful
through their birth in Strife, because their births were in anger.

> (Simplicius, *Commentary on Aristotle's Physics* 160.26)

56. (B91) <Water> has a greater affinity with wine, but with olive oil
it is unwilling <to mix>.

> (Philoponus, *Commentary on Aristotle's
> Generation of Animals* 123.19–20)

57. (B33) As when sap from a fig tree curdles and binds white milk.

> (Plutarch, *On Having Many Friends* 95A–B)

58. (B34) Having glued barley groats with water.
(Aristotle, *Meteorology* 381b31)

59. (B92) . . . like copper mixed with tin.
(Aristotle, *Generation of Animals* 2.8 747a34–b7)[8]

60. (B93) The brightness of gleaming saffron is mixed with linen.
(Plutarch, *On the Obsolescence of Oracles* 433b)

61. (B81) Wine is water from grape skin fermented in wood.
(Plutarch, *Natural Phenomena* 912b–c)

62. (B27) There neither the swift limbs of the sun are discerned,
nor the shaggy force of earth nor the sea.
Thus by the dense concealment of Harmonia is held fast
a rounded sphere, exulting in its joyous solitude.
(Plutarch, *On the Face in the Moon* 926E; Simplicius,
Commentary on Aristotle's Physics 1183.24)

63. (B27a) No dissent or unseemly battle in its limbs.
(Plutarch, *Philosophers and Princes* 777c)

64. (B28) But equal to itself on all sides, and wholly without limit,
a rounded sphere, exulting in its joyous solitude.
(Stobaeus, *Selections* 1.15.2)

65. (B29) For two branches do not spring from its back
nor do feet or swift knees or organs of generation,
but it was a sphere and equal to itself on all sides.
(Hippolytus, *Refutation of All Heresies* 7.19.13)

66. (B134) For he is not furnished in his limbs with a human
head.
Two branches do not spring from his back.
He has no feet, no swift knees, no hairy genitals,

---

8. Aristotle's comment: "On the question why mules are sterile, Empedocles explains that the mixture of seeds becomes thick, although the seed of both the horse and the ass is soft. For the hollow parts of each fit together with the thick parts of the other, and as a result a hard substance comes from soft ones."

but is only mind (*phrēn*), holy and indescribable,
darting through the entire *kosmos* with his swift thoughts.   5
    (Ammonius, *Commentary on Aristotle's On Interpretation* 249.1)

67. (B30) But when great Strife had been nourished in its limbs
and leapt up to its prerogatives as the time was being fulfilled,
that is established for them in turn by a broad oath . . .
    (Simplicius, *Commentary on Aristotle's Physics* 1184.12–13)

68. (B31) All the limbs of the god trembled, each in turn.
    (Simplicius, *Commentary on Aristotle's Physics* 1184.3)

69. (B90) Thus sweet caught hold of sweet, bitter rushed toward
    bitter,
sour went to sour, and hot coupled with hot.
    (Plutarch, *Table Talk* 4.1.3 663A;
    Macrobius, *Saturnalia* 7.5.17–18)

70. (B38) But come, I shall first tell you the beginning . . .
from which all that we now look upon came to be clear—
earth and the sea with many waves and moist air
and the Titan Aithēr, squeezing all things round about in a circle.
    (Clement, *Miscellanies* 5.48.3)

71. (B53, B54) For it sometimes happened to run this way, but often
    otherwise. . . .
Aithēr sank beneath the deep-rooted earth.
    (Aristotle, *On Generation and Corruption* 2.6 334a1–5)

72. (B44) <The sun> shines back toward Olympus with fearless face.
    (Plutarch, *On the Oracles at Delphi* 400B)

73. (B42) <The moon> keeps off the sunlight
when it goes above and darkens a portion of the earth
the size of the breadth of the gray-eyed moon.
    (Plutarch, *On the Face in the Moon* 929CD)

74. (B47) For <the moon> gazes straight at the pure circle of her lord
    [i.e., the sun].
    (Anonymous, *Useful Expressions, Anecdota Graeca* 1.337.13)

75. (B43) Thus the sunlight, having struck the broad circle of the moon . . .

> (Plutarch, *On the Face in the Moon* 929E)

76. (B45) A round alien light spins around the earth.

> (Achilles, *Introduction to Aratus* p.16 43.2–6)

77. (B46) It spins <around the earth> like the track of a chariot, and around the extremity it . . .

> (Plutarch, *On the Face in the Moon* 925B)

78. (B48) Earth makes night by obstructing <the sun's> rays.

> (Plutarch, *Platonic Questions* 1006e)

79. (B94) In the depths of a river, a dark color arises from the shadow,
and is observed as well in deep caves.

> (Plutarch, *Natural Phenomena* 39)

80. (B55) The sea is the earth's sweat.

> (Aristotle, *Meteorology* 357a24)

81. (B56) Salt is solidified when blasted by the force of the sun.

> (Hephaiston, *Handbook* 1.3, p. 2.13)

82. (B71) If your faith in these matters were at all faint—
<about> how when water, earth, Aithēr, and sun
are mixed, as many shapes and colors of mortals came to be
as now have come to be, fitted together by Aphrodite . . .

> (Simplicius, *Commentary on Aristotle's On the Heavens* 529.28)

83. (B151) Life-giving Aphrodite.

> (Plutarch, *On Love* 756e)

84. (B73) As then Cypris, busily working on shapes moistened earth in rain,
and gave it to swift fire to strengthen . . .

> (Simplicius, *Commentary on Aristotle's On the Heavens* 530.6–7)

85. (B85) Mildly-shining flame chanced upon a little earth.

> (Simplicius, *Commentary on Aristotle's Physics* 331.3)

86. (B86) From which [the roots] divine Aphrodite fashioned tireless
   eyes.
   (Simplicius, *Commentary on Aristotle's On the Heavens* 529.21)

87. (B96) Pleasant earth in her well-made crucibles
   obtained two parts of bright Nestis out of the eight,
   and four of Hephaestus, and white bones came into being,
   fitted together by the divine glues of Harmonia.
   (Simplicius, *Commentary on Aristotle's Physics* 300.21–24)

88. (B98) Earth came together by chance in about equal
      quantity to these,
   Hephaestus and rain and all-shining Aithēr,
   anchored in the perfect harbors of Cypris,
   either a bit more or a bit less of it among more of them.
   From them blood came into being and other forms of flesh.   5
      (Simplicius, *Commentary on Aristotle's Physics* 32.6–10)

89. (B82) The same things become hairs and leaves and dense
      feathers of birds,
   and scales on stout limbs.
   (Aristotle, *Meteorology* 397b4)

90. (Empedocles fr. 152 in Wright's edition)
   For all of them that exist with closely-packed roots below,
   flourishing with more widely spaced shoots.
   (Herodian, *Universal Prosody;* not in DK)

91. (B75) . . . all of them that are dense within, while their exterior
      parts
   are formed in a loose texture,
   because they met with such moisture through the devices of
      Cypris.
   (Simplicius, *Commentary on Aristotle's On the Heavens* 530.9–10)

92. (B83) . . . but in hedgehogs
   sharp-pointed hairs bristle on their backs.
   (Plutarch, *On Chance* 98D)

93. (B79) In this way tall trees first lay eggs in the form of olives.
   (Aristotle, *Generation of Animals* 731a4)

94. (B80) Therefore pomegranates and succulent apples are
       produced late
    in the season.

(Plutarch, Table Talk 683d)

95. (B62) Come now, hear how, as fire was being separated,
    it raised up the nocturnal shoots of men and women, full of
       wailing.
    For the story is not off the point or ignorant.
    First the whole-natured forms rose up out of the earth,
    having a portion of both water and heat.   5
    These the fire sent up, desiring to come to its like,
    and they did not yet show at all the lovely shape of limbs
    or a voice or the member native to men.

(Simplicius, Commentary on Aristotle's Physics 381.29)

96. (B64) Indeed, longing for sexual intercourse comes upon him
    through sight.

(Plutarch, Natural Phenomena 917c)

97. (B66) Divided meadows of Aphrodite.[9]

(Scholium on Euripides, Phoenician Women line 18)

98. (B65) They were poured in clean <places>. Some,
    encountering cold, become women.

(Aristotle, Generation of Animals 723a24)

99. (B67) That which has to do with males came to be in the warmer
       part of the earth,
    and this is why men are dark and have stronger limbs
    and more hair.

(Galen, Commentary on Hippocrates' Epidemics 6, 2.46)

100. (B68) On the tenth day of the eighth month <the blood> becomes
       white pus.

(Aristotle, Generation of Animals 4.8 777a7)

9. Translator's note: A "disgraceful" expression used of the female genitalia,
according to the source.

101. (B35) But I shall return to that path of songs
that I recounted before, drawing off this account from
   another one.
When Strife had reached the lowest depth
of the vortex, and Love comes to be in the middle of the
   whirl,
at this point all these things come together to be one single
   thing,   5
not at once, but willingly combining, different ones from
   different places.
As they were being mixed, myriads of tribes of mortal
   things poured forth,
but many remained unmixed alternately with those that
   were being mingled—
all that Strife still held back aloft. For it had not
entirely completed its blameless retreat from them to the
   furthest limits of the circle,   10
but some of its limbs remained, while others had departed.
But however far it kept running out ahead, there followed
   in pursuit
the gentle immortal onset of blameless Love.
And immediately things grew to be mortal that formerly
   had learned to be immortal,
and things previously unmixed <grew to be> mixed,
   interchanging their paths.   15
And as they were mixed, myriads of tribes of mortal things
   poured forth,
joined closely together with all kinds of forms, a wonder to
   behold.

> (Simplicius, *Commentary on Aristotle's On*
> *the Heavens* 529.1–15 [lines 1–15]; *Commentary on*
> *Aristotle's Physics* 32.13–33.2 [lines 3–17])

102. (B36) And when they were coming together, Strife was retreating
   to the extremity.

> (Stobaeus, *Selections* 1.10.11)

103. (B57) By her [Love] many neckless faces sprouted,
and arms were wandering naked, bereft of shoulders,
and eyes were roaming alone, in need of foreheads.
(Simplicius, *Commentary on Aristotle's
On the Heavens* 586.12; 587.1–2)

104. (B58) [In this situation, the limbs were still] single-limbed
[as the result of the separation caused by Strife, and] they
wandered about [aiming at mixture with one another.]
(Simplicius, *Commentary on Aristotle's On the Heavens* 587.18–19)

105. (B60) Wobbly-footed with countless hands.
(Plutarch, *Against Colotes* 1123B)

106. (B61) Many grew with faces and chests on both sides,
man-faced ox-progeny, and some to the contrary rose up
as ox-headed things with the form of men, compounded partly
from men
and partly from women, fitted with shadowy parts.
(Aelian, *The Nature of Animals* 16.29)

107. (B59) But when divinity was mixed to a greater extent with
divinity,
these things began to fall together, however they chanced to
meet,
and many others in addition arose continuously.
(Simplicius, *Commentary on Aristotle's On the Heavens* 587.20, 23)

108. (B88) A single sight [visual impression] comes from both [eyes].
(Aristotle, *Poetics* 1458a4–5)

109. (B84, B87)[10]
As when someone planning for a journey prepares a lamp,
a flame of blazing fire in the wintry night,
attaching lantern-screens to protect it from all kinds of winds,
scattering the blast of the blowing winds,
but the light springs out, since it is finer,   5
and shines across the threshold with unwearying beams,

---

10. McKirahan, the translator, has adopted Rashed's reconstruction.

in the same way, after Aphrodite had enclosed the primeval
   fire
in membranes and equipped it with pegs of love,
she poured round-eyed Kore in fine-textured garments
that keep back the depth of water that flows around   10
but let the fire pass through since it is finer,
where they are pierced through with marvelous funnels.
                    (Aristotle, *On the Senses and Their Objects* 2
                    437b24–438a5; Simplicius, *Commentary on*
                    Aristotle's On the Heavens 529.21 [line 8])

110. (B99) Fleshy twig [what Empedocles called the ear].
                    (Theophrastus, *On Sensation* 9)

111. (B100) This is how all inhale and exhale: in all of them
   bloodless
tubes of flesh extend deep in the body.
At the mouths of the tubes, the furthest extremities of the
   nostrils
are pierced through with closely arranged holes, so that
   they retain the
blood, but a clear path for Aithēr is cut through.   5
Then whenever the delicate blood leaps back from there
the bubbling air leaps in with a raging swell,
and when it [the blood] springs up, the animal exhales
   again, as when a young girl
playing with a clepsydra of shining bronze
puts the passage of the pipe against her pretty hand   10
and dunks it into the delicate body of silvery water,
no liquid enters the vessel, but the bulk of air,
pressing from inside on the close-set holes, keeps it out
until she uncovers the compressed stream. But then
when the air is leaving, the water duly enters.   15
In the same way, when water occupies the vessel and the
   bronze
mouth and passage is blocked by mortal flesh,
the air striving eagerly to get in from without restrains the
   liquid,
commanding the approaches around the gates of the
   gurgling strainer,

until she removes her hand. At that point again, in reverse
   order,   20
as the air enters, the water duly runs out.
In the same way, when delicate blood in violent motion
   through the limbs
springs backward to the inmost recesses,
immediately a stream of air raging in a swell comes in,
and when the blood swells up, it exhales an equal amount
   back again.   25
                            (Aristotle, *On Respiration* 473a15)

112. (B101) Hunting with its nostrils the fragments of animals' limbs . . .
   which they were leaving behind from their feet on the soft
   grass . . .
                    (Plutarch, *On Being a Busybody* 520e; *Natural Phenomena*
                            917e; Pseudo-Alexander, *Problems* 3.102)

113. (B102) So in this way all things have obtained both breathing and
   the sense of smell.
                            (Theophrastus, *On Sensation* 22)

114. (B104) And to the extent that they happened to fall together
   at great intervals . . . [or, "the finest things happened to fall
   together"].
                    (Simplicius, *Commentary on Aristotle's Physics* 331.41)

115. (B109) For by earth we see earth, by water, water,
   by Aithēr, divine Aithēr, and by fire, destructive fire,
   yearning by yearning, and strife by mournful strife.
                            (Aristotle, *On the Soul* 1.2 404b11–15)

116. (B110) If you fix them in your strong intelligence
   and gaze upon them propitiously with pure attention,
   these things will all be very much present to you all your
      life long,
   and from them you will obtain many others. For these very
      things
   grow into each kind of character, depending on each
      person's nature.   5

But if you reach out for other kinds of things, such as the
    millions
of wretched things that are found among men that blunt
    their thoughts,
indeed they will quickly leave you as time revolves,
longing to come to their own dear kind.
For know that all things possess thought and a portion of
    intelligence.   10
           (Hippolytus, *Refutation of All Heresies* 7.29.25)

117. (B106) Wisdom grows in humans in relation to what is present.
           (Aristotle, *On the Soul* 3.4 427a21–23)

118. (B107) For from these [the roots] all things are joined and
    compounded,
and by these they think and feel pleasure and pain.
           (Theophrastus, *On Sensation* 10)

119. (B105) <The heart is> nurtured in the seas of rebounding blood,
where most especially is what is called thought by humans,
for the blood around the heart in humans is thought.
         (Porphyry, quoted by Stobaeus in *Selections* 1.49.53)

120. (B108) Insofar as they change and become different, so far
are different thoughts always present to them.
           (Aristotle, *Metaphysics* 1009b19)

Suggestions for Further Reading

All of these entries have further bibliographies. Complete bibliographical information for collections may be found in the bibliography in
the Introduction, pp. 10–12. See also the relevant chapters in Barnes;
Guthrie; McKirahan; and Kirk, Raven, and Schofield. The volume edited
by Pierris (below) contains interesting new work on Empedocles.

Curd, P. 2001. "A New Empedocles? Implications of the Strasburg Fragments for
    Presocratic Philosophy." *Proceedings of the Boston Area Colloquium in Ancient
    Philosophy* 17: pp. 27–50.
———. "On the Question of Religion and Natural Philosophy in Empedocles,"
    in Pierris, pp. 137–62.

————. "Where Are Love and Strife? Incorporeality in Empedocles." Forthcoming in *Early Greek Philosophy: Reason at the Beginning of Philosophy*.

Gemelli-Marciano, L. "Empedocles' Zoogony and Embryology," in Pierris, pp. 373–404.

Graham, D. W. "Empedocles and Anaxagoras: Responses to Parmenides," in Long, pp. 159–80.

Inwood, B. 2001. *The Poem of Empedocles*, 2nd edition. Toronto: University of Toronto Press.

Kahn, C. "Religion and Natural Philosophy in Empedocles' Doctrine of the Soul," in Mourelatos, pp. 436–56.

Kingsley, P. 1995. *Ancient Philosophy, Mystery, and Magic*. Oxford: Clarendon Press.

Long, A. A. "Empedocles' Cosmic Cycle in the Sixties," in Mourelatos, pp. 397–425.

Martin, A., and O. Primavesi. 1999. *L'Empédocle de Strasbourg*. Berlin and New York: Walter de Gruyter.

McKirahan, R. "Assertion and Argument in Empedocles' Cosmology: Or, What Did Empedocles Learn from Parmenides?" in Pierris, pp. 163–88.

O'Brien, D. 1969. *Empedocles' Cosmic Cycle*. Cambridge: Cambridge University Press.

Osborne, C. "Sin and Moral Responsibility in Empedocles' Cosmic Cycle," in Pierris, pp. 283–308.

Parry, R. 2008. "Empedocles." In *The Stanford Encyclopedia of Philosophy (Fall 2008 Edition)*, edited by Edward N. Zalta. http://plato.stanford.edu/archives/fall2008/entries/empedocles/.

Pierris, A., ed. 2005. *The Empedoclean Kosmos: Structure, Process, and the Question of Cyclicity*. Patras: Institute for Philosophical Research.

————. 2005. "Reconstruction of Empedocles' Poem," in Pierris, ed., Appendix, pp. II–XC.

Primavesi, O. 2008. "Empedocles: Physical and Mythical Divinity," in Curd and Graham, pp. 250–83.

Rashed, M. 2007. "The Structure of the Eye and its Cosmological Function," in S. Stern-Gillet and K. Corrigan, eds., *Reading Ancient Texts, vol. 1, Presocratics and Plato*. Leiden and Boston: Brill, pp. 21–39.

Sedley, D. "Empedocles' Life Cycles," in Pierris, pp. 331–71.

Trépanier, S. 2003. "Empedocles on the Ultimate Symmetry of the World." *Oxford Studies in Ancient Philosophy* 24: pp. 1–57.

Wright, M. R. "Empedocles," in Taylor, pp. 175–207.

————. 1981, 1995. *Empedocles: The Extant Fragments*. New Haven: Yale University Press; Indianapolis: Hackett.

9. ANAXAGORAS OF CLAZOMENAE

Although Presocratic thinkers after Parmenides had their own views and theories about many of the traditional subjects, they were faced with the problem of how to reconcile giving a successful rational account of the changing world of sense experience with Parmenides' arguments against coming-to-be and passing-away and his requirements for genuine being. Anaxagoras of Clazomenae proposed one of the most intriguing of these theories. Like the earlier Ionians he had an interest in explaining the cosmos, but that interest was tempered by an awareness of the metaphysical implications of the work of Parmenides. (As in Empedocles, some of the passages in Anaxagoras are echoes of Parmenides.) Anaxagoras was born in Clazomenae, in Ionia, probably around 500 BCE. He went to Athens, the first of the early Greek philosophers to live there, and spent about thirty years in the city, where he became an associate of Pericles, the politician. He was said to have predicted the fall of a meteorite at Aegospotami in 467. This is no doubt connected with his view that the sun and the other stars are fiery stones that are snatched up from the surface of the earth by the force of the revolving mass of ingredients and sometimes fall back to earth when shaken loose from their orbits. His political associations combined with his nonconformist views (he said that the heavenly bodies are stones and that none is a god) resulted in his being prosecuted for impiety, a charge the Athenians would later make against both Socrates and Aristotle. Convicted, Anaxagoras was exiled from the city and went to Lampsacus, in northern Ionia. He was much revered in that city, and died there in about 428. According to Aristotle, Anaxagoras was older than Empedocles, but his work became known later than Empedocles' did.

Anaxagoras envisions an original state of the cosmos in which, as he says, "All things were together." All things except Mind (Nous), which is pure and unmixed, and which knows and controls all things. At some point Nous sets the original mixture of ingredients into motion: a rotation begins, and spreads out through the unlimited mass of ingredients. As a result, ingredients begin to be separated and recombined with one another, eventually producing the world that we perceive. The details of Anaxagoras' theory are controversial,

*but it is clear that he thinks that it is ingredients that are basic rather
than perceptible objects such as human beings, geological formations like
mountains, plants, and other animals, which are temporary emergences from
the mixture of ingredients.*

Note on the texts: The translations of the fragments and testimonia
given here are slightly revised versions of those by Patricia Curd in
Anaxagoras of Clazomenae.

1. (59B1) All things were together, unlimited both in amount and
    in smallness, for the small, too, was unlimited. And because all
    things were together, nothing was evident on account of smallness;
    for air and Aithēr dominated all things, both being unlimited, for
    these are the greatest among all things both in amount and in
    largeness.
    (Simplicius, *Commentary on Aristotle's Physics* 155.26–30)

2. (B2) . . . for both air and Aithēr are being separated off from the sur-
    rounding mass, and what is surrounding is unlimited in extent.
    (Simplicius, *Commentary on Aristotle's Physics* 155.31–156.1)

3. (B3) Nor of the small is there a smallest, but always a smaller (for
    what-is cannot not be)—but also of the large there is always a
    larger. And [the large] is equal to the small in extent (*plēthos*), but
    in relation to itself each thing is both large and small.
    (Simplicius, *Commentary on Aristotle's Physics* 155.26–30)

4. (B4) Since these things are so, it is right to think that there are
    many different things present in everything that is being com-
    bined, and seeds of all things, having all sorts of forms, colors,
    and flavors, and that humans and also the other animals were
    compounded, as many as have soul. Also that there are cities that
    have been constructed by humans and works made, just as with
    us, and that there are a sun and a moon and other heavenly bod-
    ies for them, just as with us, and the earth grows many different
    things for them, the most valuable of which they gather together
    into their household and use. I have said this about the separation
    off, because there would be separation off not only for us but also

elsewhere. . . . Before there was separation off, because all things were together, there was not even any color evident; for the mixture of all things prevented it, of the wet and the dry and of the hot and the cold and of the bright and the dark, and there was much earth present and seeds unlimited in number, in no way similar to one another. For no one of the others is similar to another. Since these things are so, it is right to think that all things were present in the whole.

(Simplicius, *Commentary on Aristotle's Physics* 34.29–35.9, 34.21–26)

5. (B5) Even though these things have been dissociated in this way, it is right to recognize that all things are in no way less or more (for it is impossible that they be more than all), but all things are always equal.

(Simplicius, *Commentary on Aristotle's Physics* 156.10–12)

6. (B6) Since the shares of the large and the small are equal in number, in this way too, all things will be in everything; nor is it possible that [anything] be separate, but all things have a share of everything. Since it is not possible that there is a least, it would not be possible that [anything] be separated, nor come to be by itself, but just as in the beginning, now too all things are together. In all things there are many things present, equal in number, both in the greater and in the lesser of the things being separated off.

(Simplicius, *Commentary on Aristotle's Physics* 164.26–165.1)

7. (B7) . . . so as not to know the extent of the things being separated off, either in word or in deed.

(Simplicius, *Commentary on Aristotle's On the Heavens* 608.26)

8. (B8) The things in the one *kosmos* have not been separated from one another, nor hacked apart with an axe—neither the hot from the cold nor the cold from the hot.

(Simplicius, *Commentary on Aristotle's Physics* 175.12–14; 176.29)

9. (B9) . . . as these things are revolving in this way and being separated off by force and swiftness, the swiftness produces force; and their swiftness resembles the swiftness of nothing that is now present among humans, but is altogether many times as fast.

(Simplicius, *Commentary on Aristotle's Physics* 35.14–18)

10. (B10) For how . . . can hair come from what is not hair, and flesh from what is not flesh?
    (Scholium on Gregory of Nazianzus, *Patrologia Graeca* 36.911)

11. (B11) In everything there is a share of everything except *Nous* (Mind), but there are some things in which *Nous*, too, is present.
    (Simplicius, *Commentary on Aristotle's Physics* 164.22)

12. (B12) The other things have a share of everything, but *Nous* is unlimited and self-ruling and has been mixed with no thing, but is alone itself by itself. For if it were not by itself, but had been mixed with anything else, then it would partake of all things, if it had been mixed with anything (for there is a share of everything in everything, just as I have said before); and the things mixed together with it would thwart it, so that it would control none of the things in the way that it in fact does, being alone by itself. For it is the finest of all things and the purest, and indeed it maintains all discernment (*gnōmē*) about everything and has the greatest strength. And *Nous* has control over all things that have soul, both the larger and the smaller. And *Nous* controlled the whole revolution, so that it started to revolve in the beginning. First it began to revolve from a small region, but it is revolving yet more, and it will revolve still more. And *Nous* knew (*egnō*) them all: the things that are being mixed together, the things that are being separated off, and the things that are being dissociated. And whatever sorts of things were going to be, and whatever sorts were and now are not, and as many as are now and whatever sorts will be, all these *Nous* set in order. And *Nous* also ordered this revolution, in which the things being separated off now revolve, the stars and the sun and the moon and the air and the Aithēr. This revolution caused them to separate off. The dense is being separated off from the rare, and the warm from the cold, and the bright from the dark, and the dry from the moist. But there are many shares of many things; nothing is completely separated off or dissociated one from the other except *Nous*. All *Nous* is alike, both the greater and the smaller. Nothing else is like anything else, but each one is and was most manifestly those things of which there are the most in it.
    (Simplicius, *Commentary on Aristotle's Physics* 164.24–25, 156.13–157.4)

13. (B13) When *Nous* began to move [things], there was separation off from the multitude that was being moved, and whatever *Nous* moved, all this was dissociated; and as things were being moved and dissociated, the revolution made them dissociate much more.
(Simplicius, *Commentary on Aristotle's Physics* 300.31–301.1)

14. (B14) *Nous*, which always is, most assuredly is even now where all the other things also are, in the surrounding multitude, and in the things that were joined together and in the things that have been separated off.
(Simplicius, *Commentary on Aristotle's Physics* 157.7–9)

15. (B15) The dense and the wet and the cold and the dark came together here, where <the> earth is now; but the rare and the hot and the dry <and the bright> moved out to the far reaches of the Aithēr.
(Simplicius, *Commentary on Aristotle's Physics* 179.3–6)

16. (B16) From these, as they are being separated off, earth is compacted; for water is separated off from the clouds, and earth from the water, and from the earth stones are compacted by the cold, and these stones move farther out than the water.
(Simplicius, *Commentary on Aristotle's Physics* 179.8–10; 155.21–23)

17. (B17) The Greeks do not think correctly about coming-to-be and passing-away; for no thing comes to be or passes away, but is mixed together and dissociated from the things that are. And thus they would be correct to call coming-to-be mixing-together and passing-away dissociating.
(Simplicius, *Commentary on Aristotle's Physics* 163.20–24)

18. (B18) The sun places the light in the moon.
(Plutarch, *On the Face in the Moon* 929b)

19. (B19) We call the reflection of the sun in the clouds a rainbow.
(Scholium on *Iliad* 17.547)

20. (B21) Owing to their [the senses'] feebleness, we are not able to determine the truth.
(Sextus Empiricus, *Against the Mathematicians* 7.90)

21. (B21a) Appearances are a sight of the unseen . . .
>   (Sextus Empiricus, *Against the Mathematicians* 7.140)

22. (B22) . . . egg whites are bird's milk.
>   (Athenaeus, *Sophists at Dinner* 2.57B)

23. (A102) But in all these [physical skills that animals possess] we are more unfortunate than the beasts, but by experience and memory and wisdom and art according to Anaxagoras, we make use of their activity (?) and take their honey and milk them and herding them together, use them as we will. There is nothing of chance here, but all is wisdom and forethought.[1]
>   (Plutarch, *On Fortune* 3 98F)

24. (A52) Anaxagoras probably supposed [the principles] to be unlimited in this way because he accepted as true the common opinion of the physicists that nothing comes to be from what is not. That is why they say: "all things were together," and why Anaxagoras makes the generation of a thing of a certain sort into alteration.
>   (Aristotle, *Physics* 1.4 187a23–b6)

25. (A43) Anaxagoras says just the opposite of Empedocles about the elements. For [Empedocles] claims that fire and earth, and things of the same rank, are elements of bodies and that all things are compounded of them; but Anaxagoras says the opposite. For he claims that the homogeneous stuffs are elements—I mean, for instance, flesh and bone and each of the things of that sort—and that air and fire are mixtures of them and of all the other seeds; for each of them is a collection of all the invisible homogeneous stuffs.
>   (Aristotle *On the Heavens* 3.3 302a28)

26. (A46) [Anaxagoras] makes the homogeneous stuffs elements, for instance, bone and flesh and marrow and the others of which the part is called by the same name [as the whole].
>   (Aristotle, *On Coming to Be and Passing Away* I.1 314a18)

---

1. This phrase was given by DK as B21b. Following other scholars, I think it more likely that the passage is a testimonium. There are textual problems here; I read *sphōn ti* instead of *te*.

27. (A58) When someone said that *Nous* is present—in nature just as it is in animals—as the cause of the *kosmos* and of all its order, he appeared as a sober man among the random chatterers who preceded him. We know that Anaxagoras clearly held these views, but Hermotimus of Clazomenae gets the credit for holding them earlier.

(Aristotle, *Metaphysics* I.3.984b15)

28. (A117) Anaxagoras and Empedocles say that plants are moved by desire, and they also assert that they sense and can be made sad and happy. Anaxagoras said that they are animals and feel joy and sadness, taking the fall of their leaves as evidence. . . .

([Aristotle], *On Plants* I.1.815a15)

Suggestions for Further Reading

All of these entries have further bibliographies. Complete bibliographical information for collections may be found in the bibliography in the Introduction, pp. 10–12. See also the relevant chapters in Barnes; Guthrie; McKirahan; and Kirk, Raven, and Schofield.

Curd, P. "Anaxagoras and the Theory of Everything," in Curd and Graham, pp. 230–49.

———. 2007. *Anaxagoras of Clazomenae: Fragments. Text and Translation with Notes and Essays.* Toronto: University of Toronto Press.

Furley, D. J. 1976. "Anaxagoras in Response to Parmenides." In *New Essays in Plato and the Pre-Socratics,* edited by R. A. Shiner and J. King-Farlow. *Canadian Journal of Philosophy Supplementary Volume* 2: pp. 61–85.

———. 2002. "Anaxagoras, Plato, and the Naming of Parts," in Caston and Graham, pp. 119–26.

Furth, M. 1991. "A 'Philosophical Hero'? Anaxagoras and the Eleatics." *Oxford Studies in Ancient Philosophy* 9: pp. 95–129.

Graham, D. W. 1994. "The Postulates of Anaxagoras." *Apeiron* 27: pp. 77–121.

———. "Empedocles and Anaxagoras: Responses to Parmenides," in Long, pp. 159–80.

———. 2004. "Was Anaxagoras a Reductionist?" *Ancient Philosophy* 24: pp. 1–18.

Inwood, B. 1986. "Anaxagoras and Infinite Divisibility." *Illinois Classical Studies* 11: pp. 17–33.

Laks. A. 1993. "Mind's Crisis: On Anaxagoras' NOUS." *The Southern Journal of Philosophy* 31, Supplementary Volume: pp. 19–38.

———. "Soul, Sensation, and Thought," in Long, pp. 250–70.

Lesher, J. H. 1995. "Mind's Knowledge and Powers of Control in Anaxagoras DK B12." *Phronesis* 40: pp. 125–42.

Schofield, M. 1980. *An Essay on Anaxagoras.* Cambridge: Cambridge University Press.

———. 1996. "Anaxagoras' Other World Revisited." In *Polyhistor: Studies in the History and Historiography of Ancient Philosophy,* edited by K. Algra, P. Van der Horst, and D. T. Runia, pp. 3–20. Leiden: Brill.

Sider, D. 2005. *The Fragments of Anaxagoras: Edited with an Introduction and Commentary,* 2nd edition. Sankt Augustin: Academia Verlag.

Stokes, M. C. 1965. "On Anaxagoras." *Archiv für Geschichte der Philosophie* 47: "Part I: Anaxagoras' Theory of Matter," pp. 1–19; "Part II: The Order of Cosmogony," pp. 217–50.

Strang, C. 1963. "The Physical Theory of Anaxagoras." *Archiv für Geschichte der Philosophie* 45: pp. 101–18.

Taylor, C. C. W. "Anaxagoras and the Atomists," in Taylor, pp. 208–43.

Vlastos, G. 1950, 1995. "The Physical Theory of Anaxagoras." *Philosophical Review* 59: pp. 31–57; reprinted in G. Vlastos, *Studies in Greek Philosophy, Vol. I: The Presocratics,* edited by D. W. Graham, pp. 303–27. Princeton: Princeton University Press.

———. 1975. "One World or Many in Anaxagoras?" In *Studies in Presocratic Philosophy, Vol. II,* edited by R. E. Allen and D. Furley, pp. 354–60. London: Routledge and Kegan Paul.

10. LEUCIPPUS AND DEMOCRITUS: FIFTH-CENTURY ATOMISM

Almost nothing is known of Leucippus, who was the founding theorist of atomism. Epicurus, a post-Aristotelian philosopher who adopted certain aspects of Presocratic atomism is even said to have denied that Leucippus existed. Leucippus' birthplace is variously given as Miletus, Abdera, and Elea (Miletus and Elea could represent the Milesian and Eleatic influences on his work, and Democritus, his pupil and associate was from Abdera). It is likely that Leucippus proposed the atomic system sometime around 440 to 430 BCE, thus he is contemporary with the other post-Eleatic thinkers Anaxagoras and Empedocles as well as Melissus. Two books are attributed to Leucippus: On Mind *and* The Great World System (Makrokosmos*).*

Democritus himself says that he was young when Anaxagoras was an old man; his birth date is usually placed at about 460; he lived well into the fourth century (tradition says he lived to be about 100 years old), and so was a contemporary of Socrates, Plato, and perhaps even the young Aristotle. Democritus was born in Abdera, in Thrace, a birthplace he shares with the sophist Protagoras, but he traveled widely throughout the ancient world (later sources say he went to India, but this is doubtful). Ancient sources list about seventy titles of books by Democritus on all sorts of subjects, both philosophical (on natural philosophy, ethics, mathematics, literature, and grammar) as well as on other perhaps more popular topics: He apparently wrote books on his travels; there are also reports of treatises on medicine, farming, military science, and painting. One of his books was called The Little World System (Mikrokosmos), *in obvious homage to his teacher and associate Leucippus.*

The selections included here concentrate on atomism, the scientific and metaphysical theory begun by Leucippus and continued by Democritus. Unfortunately, very few passages from Leucippus and Democritus on atomism survive; most of the evidence we have about the view comes from

*Aristotle and the Aristotelian commentators.[1] We must keep in mind that
these reports will also involve interpretation; atomism, which is a mechanistic
theory, was the major competitor to the teleological systems of both Plato
and Aristotle. The word* atomos *in Greek means "uncuttable," and so atoms
are things that cannot be cut, split, or actually divided. The atomists claim
that there is an indefinite number of these atoms, each of which is uniform,
not subject to coming-to-be or passing-away, and unchangeable in any other
way, except position, an external change that does not affect the inner core of
atomic being. Atoms thus satisfy the Parmenidean requirements for reality.
Individual atoms are imperceptible: most of them are very small, though
Democritus may have said that there could be an atom as large as the cosmos.
All atomic stuff is the same; atoms differ from one another only in shape and
size (there is controversy about whether pre-Platonic atomists considered
weight as a property of atoms).*

*The second player in the atomic system is "the empty" (void). Void is where
the atoms are not, and atoms are able to move into the empty. The atomists
explicitly call the void "the nothing" or the "what is not," whereas atoms
are called "the something" or the "what is." Hence they explicitly challenge
Parmenides' proscription against what-is-not; yet there is good evidence that
they insisted that the void is real in its own right, and not simply the negation
of what-is. Void separates atoms, which allows them to move and come
close to one another without melding into each other. The mixing together
and separating of the different types of atoms into different arrangements
is responsible for all the aspects of the sensible world, and so what looks
like coming-to-be and passing-away is merely rearrangement of the basic
entities—atoms and void. All else is, as Democritus says, "by convention."
Democritus offered complex accounts of the structure of physical objects (i.e.,
arrangements of atoms) and of perception, thought, and knowledge, as well
as of many other aspects of human life. There are many fragments on ethical
matters attributed to him, but the authenticity of these is unclear.*

1. (67B2) No thing happens at random but all things as a result of a
reason and by necessity.[2]

(Aëtius 1.25.4)

1. Aristotle wrote a multivolume work on Democritus; only fragments survive,
thanks to Simplicius, who quotes some passages (see selection 5, below).
2. This is one of the few fragments that can be assigned to Leucippus with
some confidence. Leucippus' DK number is 67, while Democritus' is 68.

2. (67A1) Leucippus' opinion is this: All things are unlimited and they all turn around one another; the all [the universe] is both the empty [void] and the full. The worlds come to be when the atoms fall into the void and are entangled with one another. The nature of the stars comes to be from their motion, and from their increase [in entanglements]. The sun is carried around in a larger circle around the moon; and whirled around the center, the earth rides steady; its shape is drumlike. He was the first to make the atoms first principles.

> (Diogenes Laertius, *Lives of the Philosophers* 9.30; tpc)

3. (67A6) Leucippus and his associate Democritus declare the full and the empty [void] to be the elements, calling the former "what-is" (*to on*) and the other "what-is-not" (*to mē on*). Of these, the one, "what-is," is full and solid, the other, "what-is-not," is empty [void] and rare. (This is why they say that what-is is no more than what-is-not, because the void is no less than body is.) These are the material causes of existing things. . . . They declare that the differences <among these> are the causes of the rest. Moreover, they say that the differences are three: shape, arrangement, and position. For they say that what-is differs only in "rhythm," "touching," and "turning"—and of these "rhythm" is shape, "touching" is arrangement, and "turning" is position. For *A* differs from *N* in shape, *AN* from *NA* in arrangement, and *Z* from *N* in position. Concerning the origin and manner of motion in existing things, these men too, like the rest, lazily neglected to give an account.

> (Aristotle, *Metaphysics* 1.4 985b4–20)

4. (67A9) After establishing the shapes, Democritus and Leucippus base their account of alteration and coming-to-be on them: coming-to-be and perishing by means of separation and combination, alteration by means of arrangement and position. Since they held that the truth is in the appearance, and appearances are opposite and infinite, they made the shapes infinite, so that by reason of changes of the composite, the same thing seems opposite to different people, and it shifts position when a small additional amount is mixed in, and it appears completely different when a single thing shifts position. For tragedy and comedy come to be out of the same letters.

> (Aristotle, *On Generation and Corruption* 1.1 315b6–15)

5. (68A37) Democritus believes that the nature of the eternal things is small substances (*ousiai*)[3] infinite in number. As a place for these he hypothesizes something else, infinite in size, and he calls their place by the names "the void," "not-hing" (*ouden*) and "the unlimited" [or, "infinite"] and he calls each of the substances "hing" (*den*) and "the compact" and "what-is." He holds that the substances are so small that they escape our senses. They have all kinds of forms and shapes and differences in size. Out of these as elements he generates and forms visible and perceptible bodies. <These substances> are at odds with one another and move in the void because of their dissimilarity and the other differences I have mentioned, and as they move they strike against one another and become entangled in a way that makes them be in contact and close to one another but does not make any thing out of them that is truly one, for it is quite foolish <to think> that two or more things could ever come to be one. The grounds he gives for why the substances stay together up to a point are that the bodies fit together and hold each other fast. For some of them are rough, some are hooked, others concave, and others convex, while yet others have innumerable other differences. So he thinks that they cling to each other and stay together until some stronger necessity comes along from the environment and shakes them and scatters them apart. He describes the generation and its contrary, separation, not only for animals but also for plants, *kosmoi*, and altogether for all perceptible bodies.

> (Aristotle, *On Democritus*, quoted by Simplicius, *Commentary on Aristotle's On the Heavens* 295.1–22)

6. (67A8, 68A38) Leucippus . . . did not follow the same route as Parmenides and Xenophanes concerning things that are, but seemingly the opposite one. For while they made the universe one, immovable, ungenerated, and limited, and did not even permit the investigation of what-is-not, he posited the atoms as infinite and ever-moving elements, with an infinite number of shapes, on the grounds that they are no more like this than like that and because he observed that coming-to-be and change are unceasing among the things that are. Further, he posited that what-is is no more

---

3. Translator's note: *Ousia*, "substance," is a noun derived from the verb *einai*, "to be." There is a connection in language and meaning between *ousia* and *on*.

than what-is-not, and both are equally causes of things that come to be. For supposing the substance of the atoms to be compact and full, he said it is what-is and that it moves in the void, which he called "what-is-not" and which he declares is no less than what-is. His associate, Democritus of Abdera, likewise posited the full and the void as principles, of which he calls the former "what-is" and the latter "what-is-not." For positing the atoms as matter for the things that are, they generate the rest by means of their differences. These are three: rhythm, turning, and touching, that is, shape, position, and arrangement. For by nature like is moved by like, and things of the same kind move toward one another, and each of the shapes produces a different condition when arranged in a different combination. Thus, since the principles are infinite, they reasonably promised to account for all attributes and substances—how and through what cause anything comes to be. This is why they say that only those who make the elements infinite account for everything reasonably. They say that the number of the shapes among the atoms is infinite on the grounds that they are no more like this than like that. For they themselves assign this as a cause of the infiniteness.

(Simplicius, *Commentary on Aristotle's Physics* 28.4–26)

7. (67A7) Leucippus and Democritus have accounted for all things very systematically and in a single theory, taking the natural starting point as their own. For some of the early philosophers held that what-is is necessarily one and immovable. For the void is not, and motion is impossible without a separate void, nor can there be many things without something to keep them apart. . . . But Leucippus thought he had arguments that assert what is generally granted to perception, not abolishing coming-to-be, perishing, motion, or plurality. Agreeing on these matters with the phenomena and agreeing with those who support the one [that is, the Eleatics] that there could be no motion without void, he asserts that void is what-is-not and that nothing of what-is is not, since what strictly is is completely full. But this kind of thing is not one thing but things that are infinite in number and invisible because of the minuteness of their size. These move in the void (for there is void), and they produce coming-to-be by combining and perishing by coming apart, and they act and are acted upon wherever they happen to come into contact (for in this way they are not one), and they

generate <compounds> by becoming combined and entangled. A plurality could not come to be from what is in reality one, nor one from what is really many, but this is impossible.

(Aristotle, *On Generation and Corruption* 1.8 324b35–325a36)

8. (67A19) They declare that their [atoms'] nature is but one, as if each one were a separate piece of gold.

(Aristotle, *On the Heavens* 1.7 275b32–276a1)

9. (68A59) Plato and Democritus supposed that only the intelligible things are true (or, "real"); Democritus <held this view> because there is by nature no perceptible substrate, since the atoms, which combine to form all things, have a nature deprived of every perceptible quality.

(Sextus Empiricus, *Against the Mathematicians* 8.6)

10. (68A47) Democritus specified two <basic properties of atoms>: size and shape; and Epicurus added weight as a third.

(Aëtius 1.3.18)

11. (67A15) Since the bodies differ in shape, and the shapes are infinite, they declare the simple bodies to be infinite too. But they did not determine further what is the shape of each of the elements, beyond assigning a spherical shape to fire. They distinguished air and water and the others by largeness and smallness.

(Aristotle, *On the Heavens* 3.4 303a11–15)

12. (67A14) These men [Leucippus, Democritus, and Epicurus] said that the principles are infinite in multitude, and they believed them to be atoms and indivisible and incapable of being affected because they are compact and have no share of void. (For they claimed that division occurs where there is void in bodies.)

(Simplicius, *Commentary on Aristotle's On the Heavens* 242.18–21)

13. (67A13) Those who abandoned division to infinity on the grounds that we cannot divide to infinity and as a result cannot guarantee that the division cannot end, declared that bodies are composed of indivisible things and are divided into indivisibles. Except that Leucippus and Democritus hold that the cause of the primary

bodies' indivisibility is not only their inability to be affected but also their minute size and lack of parts.

(Simplicius, *Commentary on Aristotle's Physics* 925.10–15)

14. (68A48b) Democritus would appear to have been persuaded by arguments that are appropriate to the science of nature. The point will be clear as we proceed. For there is a difficulty in supposing that there is a body, a magnitude, that is everywhere divisible and that this [the complete division] is possible. For what will there be that escapes the division? . . . Now since such a body is everywhere divisible, let it be divided. What, then, will be left? A magnitude? But that cannot be. For there will be something that has not been divided, whereas we supposed that it was everywhere divisible. But if there is no body or magnitude left and yet the division will take place, either <the original body> will consist of points and its components will be without magnitude, or it will be nothing at all so that even if it were to come to be out of nothing and be composed of nothing, the whole thing would then be nothing but an appearance. Likewise, if it is composed of points it will not be a quantity. For when they were in contact and there was a single magnitude and they coincided, they made the whole thing no larger. For when it is divided into two or more, the whole is no smaller or larger than before. And so even if all the points are put together they will not make any magnitude. . . . These problems result from supposing that any body whatever of any size is everywhere divisible. . . . And so, since magnitudes cannot be composed of contacts or points, it is necessary for there to be indivisible bodies and magnitudes.

(Aristotle, *On Generation and Corruption* 1.2 316a13–b16)

15. (67A7) When Democritus said that the atoms are in contact with each other, he did not mean contact, strictly speaking, which occurs when the surfaces of the things in contact fit perfectly with one another, but the condition in which the atoms are near one another and not far apart is what he called contact. For no matter what, they are separated by void.

(Philoponus, *Commentary on Aristotle's On Generation and Corruption* 158.27–159.3)

16. (68B156) [When Democritus declares that] There is no more reason for the "hing" {Greek: *den*} to be than the nothing {Greek: *mēden*, not-hing}, [he is calling thing body and nothing void, and declaring that this too (void) has some nature and existence of its own.]
(Plutarch, *Against Colotes* 1108F; tpc)

17. (67A19) By "void" people mean an interval in which there is no perceptible body. Since they believe that everything that is is body, they say that void is that in which there is nothing at all. . . . So it is necessary to prove[4] . . . that there is no interval different from bodies . . . which breaks up the totality of body so that it is not continuous, as Democritus, Leucippus, and many other natural philosophers say, or that there is anything outside the totality of body, supposing that it is continuous. . . . They say that (1) there would be no change in place (that is, motion and growth), since it does not seem that there would be motion unless there were void, since what is full cannot admit anything else. . . . (2) Some things are seen to contract and be compressed; for example, they say that the jars hold the wine along with the wineskins, since the compressed body contracts into the empty places that are in it. Further, (3) all believe that growth takes place through void, since the nourishment is a body and two bodies cannot coincide. (4) They also use as evidence what happens with ash: it takes no less water to fill a jar that contains ashes than it does to fill the same jar when it is empty.
(Aristotle, *Physics* 4.6 213a27–b22)

18. (67A16) This is why Leucippus and Democritus, who say that the primary bodies are always moving in the void (that is, the infinite) must specify what motion they have and what is their natural motion.
(Aristotle, *On the Heavens* 3.2 300b8–11)

---

4. Translator's note: This passage forms part of Aristotle's treatment of void, in which he both presents the arguments offered in favor of the thesis that void exists and shows why they fail. Aristotle here says that he needs to refute the view that void exists.

19. (67A18) For they say that there is always motion. But why it is and what motion it is, they do not state, nor do they give the cause of its being of one sort rather than another.

(Aristotle, *Metaphysics* 12.6 1071b33–35)

20. (68A58) They say that motion occurs because of the void. For they, too, say that nature[5] undergoes motion in respect of place.

(Aristotle, *Physics* 8.9 265b24–25)

21. (67A16) Leucippus and Democritus said that their primary bodies, the atoms, are always moving in the infinite void by compulsion.

(Simplicius, *Commentary on Aristotle's On the Heavens* 583.18–20)

22. (68A47) Democritus, saying that the atoms are by nature motionless, declares that they move "by a blow."

(Simplicius, *Commentary on Aristotle's Physics* 42.10–11)

23. (68A47) Democritus says that the primary bodies (these are the compact things) do not possess weight but move by striking against one another in the infinite, and there can be an atom the size of a *kosmos*.

(Aëtius 1.12.6)

24. (67A6) These men [Leucippus and Democritus] say that the atoms move by hitting and striking against each other, but they do not specify the source of their natural motion. For the motion of striking each other is compelled and not natural, and compelled motion is posterior to natural motion.

(Alexander, *Commentary on Aristotle's Metaphysics* 36.21–25)

25. (68A58) They said that moving by virtue of the weight in them, <the atoms> move with respect to place through the void, which yields and does not resist. For they said that they "are hurled all about." And they attribute this motion to the elements as not just their primary but in fact their only motion, whereas things composed of the elements have the other kinds of motion. For they grow and decrease, change, come to be, and perish through the combination and separation of the primary bodies.

(Simplicius, *Commentary on Aristotle's Physics* 1318.35–1319.5)

---

5. Translator's note: This is a word the Atomists used to refer to the atoms.

26. (68A47) Democritus holds that there is one kind of motion, that due to pulsation.

(Aëtius 1.23.3)

27. (68A60) Those <who call the primary bodies> solid can rather say that the larger ones are heavier. But since compounds do not appear to behave in this way, and we see many that are smaller in bulk but heavier, as bronze is heavier than wood, some think and say that the cause is different—that the void enclosed within makes the bodies light and sometimes makes larger things lighter, since they contain more void. . . . Those who make these distinctions must add not only that something contains more void if it is lighter but also that it contains less solid.

(Aristotle, *On the Heavens* 4.2 309a1–14)

28. (68A66) Democritus leaves aside purpose but refers all things which nature employs to necessity.

(Aristotle, *Generation of Animals* 5.8 789b2–4)

29. (68A66) <Concerning necessity> Democritus <says it is> the knocking against <each other> and the motion and "blow" of matter.

(Aëtius 1.26.2)

30. (68A68) <Democritus> seemed to employ chance in his cosmogony, but in his detailed discussions he declares that chance is the cause of nothing, and he refers to other causes.

(Simplicius, *Commentary on Aristotle's Physics* 330.14–17)

31. (67A14) These atoms, which are separate from one another in the infinite void and differ in shape and size and position and arrangement, move in the void, and when they overtake one another they collide, and some rebound in whatever direction they may happen to, but others become entangled by virtue of the way their shapes, sizes, positions, and arrangements correspond, and they stay together, and this is how compounds are produced.

(Simplicius, *Commentary on Aristotle's
On the Heavens* 242.21–26)

32. (68A57) What does Democritus say? That atomic substances infinite in number, not different in kind, and moreover incapable of acting or being acted upon, are in motion, scattered in the void. When they approach one another or collide or become entangled, the compounds appear as water or fire or as a plant or a human, but all things are atoms, which he calls forms; there is nothing else. For there is no coming-to-be from what-is-not, and nothing could come to be from things that are, because on account of their hardness the atoms are not acted upon and do not change.

(Plutarch, *Against Colotes* 8 1110F–1111A)

33. (68B155) If a cone is cut by a plane parallel to the base, what should we think about the surfaces of the segments? Do they prove to be equal or unequal? If they are unequal they will make the cone uneven, with many step-like notches and rough spots, but if they are equal the segments will be equal, and the cone will appear to have the character of a cylinder, being composed of equal not unequal circles, which is most absurd.

(Plutarch, *Against the Stoics on Common Conceptions* 1079E)

34. (67A14) Leucippus and Democritus, calling the smallest and primary bodies atoms, <say> that by virtue of differences in their shapes and position and order, some bodies come to be hot and fiery—those composed of rather sharp and minute primary bodies situated in a similar position, while others come to be cold and watery—those composed of the opposite kinds of bodies. And some come to be bright and shining, while others come to be dim and dark.

(Simplicius, *Commentary on Aristotle's Physics* 36.1–7)

35. (68A129) He makes sweet that which is round and good-sized; astringent that which is large, rough, polygonal, and not rounded; sharp-tasting, as its name indicates, sharp and angular in body, bent, fine, and not rounded; pungent, round, small, angular, and bent; salty, angular, good-sized, crooked, and equal-sided; bitter, round, smooth, crooked, and small-sized; oily, fine, round, and small.

(Theophrastus, *Causes of Plants* 6.1.6)

36. (68A135) Iron is harder and lead is heavier, since iron has its atoms arranged unevenly and has large quantities of void in many

places . . . while lead has less void, but its atoms are arranged
evenly throughout. This is why it is heavier but softer than iron.

(Theophrastus, *On Sensation* 62)

37. (67A1) <Leucippus> declares the universe to be infinite. . . . Of this,
some is full and some is empty [void], and he declares these [full
and void] to be elements. An infinite number of *kosmoi* arise out
of these and perish into these. The *kosmoi* come into being in the
following way. Many bodies of all sorts of shapes, being cut off
from the infinite, move into a great void. They collect together
and form a single vortex. In it they strike against one another and
move around in all different ways, and they separate apart, like
to like. When they are no longer able to rotate in equilibrium, the
fine ones depart into the void outside as if sifted. The rest remain
together, become entangled, move together in unison, and form a
first spherical complex. This stands apart like a membrane, enclos-
ing all kinds of bodies in it. As these whirl around by virtue of
the resistance of the center, the surrounding membrane becomes
thin, since the adjacent atoms join the motion when they come
into contact with the vortex. And the earth came into being in this
way when the atoms moving to the center remained together. And
again the surrounding membrane-like thing itself grows because
of the accretion of bodies from outside. As it moves in a vortex
it acquires whatever it comes into contact with. Some of these
become intertwined and form a complex that is at first damp and
muddy, but when they have dried out and rotate with the vortex
of the whole, they catch fire and form the nature of the stars.

(Diogenes Laertius, *Lives of the Philosophers* 9.31–32)

38. (68B164) Animals flock together with animals of the same kind—
doves with doves, cranes with cranes, and likewise for the other
irrational kinds. It is the same for inanimate things, as can be seen
in the cases of seeds being sifted and pebbles on the shore. For
through the swirling and separating motion of the sieve, lentils
wind up together with lentils, wheat with wheat, and barley with
barley, and through the motion of the waves, elongated pebbles
are pushed to the same place as other elongated ones, and round
ones to the same place as round ones, as if the similarity in these
had some mutually attractive force for things.

(Sextus Empiricus, *Against the Mathematicians* 7.116)

39. (68A40) There are an infinite number of *kosmoi* of different sizes. In some there is no sun or moon. In some the sun and moon are larger than ours, and in others there are more. The distances between the *kosmoi* are unequal, and in one region there are more, in another fewer. Some are growing, some are at their peak, and some are declining, and here one is coming into being, there one is ceasing to be. They perish when they collide with one another. Some *kosmoi* have no animals, plants, or any moisture. In our own *kosmos* the earth came into being before the stars. The moon is lowest, then the sun, then the fixed stars. The planets too have unequal heights. A *kosmos* is at its peak until it is no longer able to take anything in from outside.

(Hippolytus, Refutation of All Heresies 1.13.2–4)

40. (67A1) The orbit of the sun is furthest out, that of the moon is nearest, and the others are in between. All the stars are on fire because of the speed of their motion; the sun too is on fire because of the stars, while the moon has only a small share of fire. The sun and moon suffer eclipses . . . [something is missing from the text—probably a reference to the ecliptic] because the earth is tilted toward the south. The regions to the north are always covered with snow and are very cold and frozen. The sun is eclipsed rarely, but the moon is eclipsed often because their orbits are unequal.

(Diogenes Laertius, Lives of the Philosophers 9.33)

41. (68A93) Democritus stated that thunder results from an uneven compound forcing the surrounding cloud to move downward. Lightning is the collision of clouds, as a result of which the atoms that generate fire are filtered through interstices containing much void (a process that involves friction) and collect in the same place. A thunderbolt occurs when there is a violent motion of fire-producing atoms that are very pure, fine, even, and "close-fitted" (the word Democritus himself uses). A waterspout occurs when compounds of fire containing much void are held back in regions with a lot of void and are wrapped in special membranes, and form bodies because of this rich mixture and make a rush toward the depth.

(Aëtius 3.3.11)

42. (68A104) Some say that the soul moves the body in which it is
found in the same way as it is itself moved: Democritus, for example, who has a view like Philippos the comic poet, who says that
Daedalus made the wooden statue of Aphrodite move by pouring
quicksilver into it. Democritus speaks similarly, since he says that
the indivisible spheres are in motion because their nature is never
to stay still, and to draw the entire body along with them and move
it. But we will ask if these same things also produce rest. How they
will do so is difficult or impossible to state. In general, the soul
does not appear to move the body in this way, but through choice
of some kind and through thought.

(Aristotle, *On the Soul* 1.3 406b16–25)

43. (68A135) The visual impression is not formed directly in the
pupil, but the air between the eye and the object is contracted and
stamped by the seen object and by the seeing thing. For there is a
continual effluence from everything. Then this [air], which is solid
and has a different color, forms an impression in the eyes, which
are moist.

(Theophrastus, *On Sensation* 50)

44. (68B9) Nonetheless [Democritus] is found condemning them [the
senses]. For he says, "We in fact understand nothing exactly [or,
"exact"], but what changes according to the disposition both of the
body and of the things that enter it and offer resistance to it."

(Sextus Empiricus, *Against the Mathematicians* 7.136)

45. (68B11) There are two kinds of judgment, one legitimate and the
other bastard. All the following belong to the bastard: sight, hearing, smell, taste, touch. The other is legitimate and is separate from
this. When the bastard one is unable to see or hear or smell or
taste or grasp by touch any further in the direction of smallness,
but <we need to go still further> toward what is fine, <then the
legitimate one enables us to carry on>.[6]

(Sextus Empiricus, *Against the Mathematicians* 7.138)

6. Translator's note: This fragment trails off into corruption, but there is general
agreement about the sense of what is missing.

46. (68B9) By convention [or, "custom"], sweet; by convention, bitter; by convention, hot; by convention, cold; by convention, color; but in reality, atoms and void.[7]

> (Sextus Empiricus, *Against the Mathematicians* 7.135)

47. (68B6) A person must know by this rule [*kanōn:* measuring stick, standard] that he is separated from reality.

> (Sextus Empiricus, *Against the Mathematicians* 7.136)

48. (68B8) In fact it will be clear that to know in reality what each thing is like is a matter of perplexity [or, "that people are at a loss to know in reality what each thing is like"].

> (Sextus Empiricus, *Against the Mathematicians* 7.136)

49. (68B7) In reality we know nothing about anything, but for each person opinion is a reshaping [of the soul-atoms by the atoms entering from without].

> (Sextus Empiricus, *Against the Mathematicians* 7.136)

50. (68A112) Either nothing is true, or at least to us it is unclear [or, "hidden"]. It is because these thinkers suppose intelligence to be sensation, and that, in turn, to be an alteration, that they say that what appears to our senses must be true (or, "real").

> (Aristotle, *Metaphysics* 4.5 1009b11–15)

51. (68B117) In reality we know nothing, for truth is in the depths.

> (Diogenes Laertius, *Lives of the Philosophers* 9.72)

52. (68B125) Wretched mind, do you take your evidence from us and then throw us down? Throwing us down is a fall[8] for you!

> (Galen, *On Medical Experience* 15.8)

53. (68B166) Democritus says that certain images of atoms approach humans, and of them some cause good and others evil, and as a

---

7. There is a variant of this fragment in Plutarch (*Against Colotes* 1110E): "Color is by convention, and sweet by convention, and combination by convention" (tpc).

8. Translator's note: The word used here is a technical term for a fall in wrestling.

result he prayed "to meet with propitious images." These are large and immense, and difficult to destroy though not indestructible. They indicate the future in advance to people when they are seen and emit voices. As a result people of ancient times, upon perceiving the appearances of these things, supposed that they are a god, though there is no other god aside from these having an indestructible nature.

(Sextus Empiricus, *Against the Mathematicians* 9.19)

54. (68B191) Cheerfulness arises in people through moderation of enjoyment and due proportion in life. Deficiencies and excesses tend to change suddenly and give rise to large movements in the soul. Souls that undergo motions involving large intervals are neither steady nor cheerful . . .

(Stobaeus, *Selections* 3.1.120)

55. (68A1) The goal of life is cheerfulness, which is not the same as pleasure . . . but the state in which the soul continues calmly and stably, disturbed by no fear or superstition or any other emotion. He also calls it "well-being" and many other names.

(Diogenes Laertius, *Lives of the Philosophers* 9.45)

56. (68B74) Accept nothing pleasant unless it is beneficial.

(Democrates, *Maxims*)

57. (68B69) To all humans the same thing is good and true, but different people find different things pleasant.

(Democrates, *Maxims*)

58. (68B214) Brave is not only he who masters the enemy but also he who masters pleasures. Some are lords of cities but slaves of women.

(Stobaeus, *Selections* 3.5.25)

59. (68B33) Nature and teaching are closely related. For teaching reshapes the person and by reshaping makes <his> nature.

(Clement, *Miscellanies* 4.151)

60. (68B189) Best for a person is to live his life being as cheerful and as little distressed as possible. This will occur if he does not make his pleasures in mortal things.

(Stobaeus, *Selections* 3.1.47)

61. (68B235) All those who make their pleasures from the belly, exceeding the right time for food, drink, or sex, have short-lived pleasures—only for as long as they eat or drink—but many pains.

(Stobaeus, *Selections* 3.18.35)

Suggestions for Further Reading

All of these entries have further bibliographies. Complete bibliographical information for collections may be found in the bibliography in the Introduction, pp. 10–12. See also the relevant chapters in Barnes; Guthrie; McKirahan; and Kirk, Raven, and Schofield.

Annas, Julia. 2002. "Democritus and Eudaimonism," in Caston and Graham, pp. 169–82.

Bailey, Cyril. 1928. *The Greek Atomists and Epicurus*. Oxford: Clarendon Press.

Balme, David. 1941. "Greek Science and Mechanism II. The Atomists." *Classical Quarterly* 35: pp. 23–8.

Barnes, J. 1984. "Reason and Necessity in Leucippus." In *Proceedings of the 1st International Congress on Democritus*, vol. 1, edited by Linos G. Benakis, pp. 141–58. Xanthi.

Berryman, Sylvia. 2008. "Ancient Atomism." In *The Stanford Encyclopedia of Philosophy (Fall 2008 Edition)*, edited by Edward N. Zalta. http://plato.stanford.edu/archives/fall2008/entries/atomism-ancient/.

———. 2008. "Democritus." In *The Stanford Encyclopedia of Philosophy (Fall 2008 Edition)*, edited by Edward N. Zalta. http://plato.stanford.edu/archives/fall2008/entries/democritus/.

———. "Democritus and the Explanatory Power of the Void," in Caston and Graham, pp. 183–94.

———. 2008. "Leucippus." In *The Stanford Encyclopedia of Philosophy (Fall 2008 Edition)*, edited by Edward N. Zalta. http://plato.stanford.edu/archives/fall2008/entries/leucippus/.

Bodnar, I. 1998. "Atomic Independence and Indivisibility." *Oxford Studies in Ancient Philosophy* 16: pp. 35–61.

Cartledge, Paul. 1999. *Democritus*. London: Routledge.

Cole, T. 1990. *Democritus and the Sources of Greek Anthropology*. Atlanta, GA: Scholars Press.

Curd, P. "Why Democritus Was Not a Skeptic," in Preus, pp. 149–69.

Furley, David J. 1967. *Two Studies in the Greek Atomists*. Princeton: Princeton University Press.

————. 1987. *The Greek Cosmologists, Vol 1: The Formation of the Atomic Theory and Its Earliest Critics*. Cambridge: Cambridge University Press.

Graham, D. W. "Leucippus' Atomism," in Curd and Graham, pp. 333–52.

Konstan, David. 1982. "Atomism and Its Heritage: Minimal Parts." *Ancient Philosophy* 2: pp. 60–75.

Mourelatos, A. P. D. 2005. "Intrinsic and Relational Properties of Atoms in the Democritean Ontology." In *Metaphysics, Soul, and Ethics: Themes from the Work of Richard Sorabji*, edited by Ricardo Salles, pp. 39–63. Oxford: Oxford University Press.

O'Brien, Denis. 1981. *Democritus, Weight and Size: An Exercise in the Reconstruction of Early Greek Philosophy, Theories of Weight in the Ancient World*, vol. 1. Leiden: E. J. Brill.

Pyle, Andrew. 1997. *Atomism and Its Critics: From Democritus to Newton*. Bristol: Thoemmes Press.

O'Keefe, T. 1997. "The Ontological Status of Sensible Qualities for Democritus and Epicurus." *Ancient Philosophy* 17: pp. 119–34.

Sedley, D. 2008. "Atomism's Eleatic Roots," in Curd and Graham, pp. 305–32.

————. 1982. "Two Conceptions of Vacuum." *Phronesis* 27: pp. 175–93.

Sorabji, Richard. 1983. *Time, Creation, and the Continuum: Theories in Antiquity and the Early Middle Ages*. London and Ithaca, NY: Duckworth and Cornell University Press.

Taylor, C. C. W. "The Atomists," in Long, pp. 181–204.

————. 1999. *The Atomists: Leucippus and Democritus. Fragments, A Text and Translation with Commentary*. Toronto: University of Toronto Press.

Vlastos, G. 1975. "Ethics and Physics in Democritus." In *Studies in Presocratic Philosophy*, vol. 2: *Eleatics and Pluralists*, edited by D. J. Furley and R. E. Allen, pp. 381–408. London: Routledge & Kegan Paul.

Wardy, Robert. 1988. "Eleatic Pluralism." *Archiv für Geschichte der Philosophie* 70: pp. 125–46.

11. MELISSUS OF SAMOS

Melissus was an admiral as well as a philosopher. Although he lived on Samos (an island in the eastern Aegean that was the birthplace of Pythagoras), he adopted Parmenides' arguments. We do not know the year of his birth, but in 441 BCE he was the admiral of a fleet that defeated the Athenians under Pericles. Melissus' treatise was a sustained exploration of the consequences of Parmenides' views, and he even extends Parmenides' arguments. Melissus argues that only one thing can be, and that among other characteristics, the One (as he called it) must be changeless and full, not subject to changes in density and rarity, not subject to rearrangement, and not subject to pain or pleasure. These arguments seemingly take on the Milesians; Anaxagoras and the Atomists, whose many ingredients change place and are rearranged (in addition, the Atomists are committed to the reality of void); and Empedocles, who has four ingredients that are rearranged, and whose divine sphere "rejoices." Melissus was roundly abused by Aristotle, who said Melissus was somewhat unrefined in his views, but Melissus sets out his arguments clearly and uses Parmenides' claims about what-is to challenge the truth of the evidence of the senses, and to call into question some basic assumptions of post-Parmenidean theories.

1. (30B1) Whatever was, always was and always will be. For if it came to be, it is necessary that before it came to be it was nothing. Now if it was nothing, in no way could anything come to be out of nothing.

    (Simplicius, *Commentary on Aristotle's Physics* 162.23–26)

2. (B2) Now since it did not come to be, it is and always was and always will be, and it does not have a beginning or an end, but it is unlimited. For if it had come to be it would have a beginning (for if it had come to be it would have begun at some time) and an

end (for if it had come to be it would have ended at some time).[1]
But since it neither began nor ended, and always was and always
will be, it does not have a beginning or end. For whatever is not
entire [or, "all"] cannot always be.
(Simplicius, *Commentary on Aristotle's Physics* 29.22–26, 109.20–25)

3. (B3) [Just as he says that what came to be at some time is limited
in its being, he also wrote clearly that what always is is unlimited
in being, saying:] But just as it always is, so also it must always be
unlimited in magnitude. [But by "magnitude" he does not mean
what is extended in space.][2]
(Simplicius, *Commentary on Aristotle's Physics* 109.29–32)

4. (B4) Nothing that has both a beginning and an end is either eternal
or unlimited.
(Simplicius, *Commentary on Aristotle's Physics* 110.2–4)

5. (B5) If it is not one, it will come to a limit in relation to something
else.
(Simplicius, *Commentary on Aristotle's Physics* 110.5–6)

6. (B6) For if it is <unlimited>, it will be one. For if there were two,
they could not be unlimited, but they would have limits in relation
to each other.
(Simplicius, *Commentary on Aristotle's On the Heavens* 557.14–17)

7. (B7) Thus it is eternal and unlimited and one and all alike.
And it cannot perish or become greater or be rearranged, nor
does it feel pain or distress. For if it underwent any of these, it
would no longer be one. For if it becomes different, it is necessary
that what-is is not alike, but what previously was perishes, and
what-is-not comes to be. Now if it were to become different by a
single hair in ten thousand years, it would all perish in the whole
of time.

---

1. Translator's note: Although a better attested manuscript reading yields the
translations "it would have begun coming to be at some time," and "it would
have ended coming to be at some time," it is difficult to make sense of these
claims.

2. Simplicius' comments are included in square brackets.

But it is not possible for it to be rearranged either. For the arrangement that previously was is not destroyed, and an arrangement that is not does not come to be. But when nothing either comes to be in addition or is destroyed or becomes different, how could there be a rearrangement of things-that-are? For if it became at all different, it would thereby have in fact been rearranged.

Nor does it feel pain. For it could not be entire [or, "all"] if it were feeling pain. For a thing feeling pain could not always be. Nor does it have equal power to what is healthy. Nor would it be alike if it were feeling pain. For it would be feeling pain because something is either being taken away or added, and it would no longer be alike.

Nor could what is healthy feel pain. For what is healthy and what-is would perish and what-is-not would come to be.

And the same argument applies to feeling distress as to feeling pain.

Nor is any of it empty.[3] For what is empty is nothing, and of course what is nothing cannot be. Nor does it move. For it cannot give way anywhere, but it is full. For if it were empty, it would give way into the empty part. But since it is not empty it has nowhere to give way.

It cannot be dense and rare. For it is impossible for the rare to be equally full as the dense, but the rare thereby proves to be emptier than the dense.

And we must make this the criterion of full and not full: If something yields or is penetrated, it is not full. But if it neither yields nor is penetrated, it is full.

Hence it is necessary that it is full if it is not empty. Hence if it is full it does not move.

(Simplicius, *Commentary on Aristotle's Physics* 111.18–112.15)

8. (B8) [After saying of what-is that it is one and ungenerated and motionless and interrupted by no void, but is a whole full of itself, he goes on:][4] Now this argument is the strongest indication that there is only one thing. But the following are indications too.

If there were many things, they must be such as I say the one is. For if there are earth and water and air and fire and iron and gold

3. The word translated "empty" can also mean "void."
4. The comment in square brackets is from Simplicius.

and the living and the dead and black and white and all the other things that people say are real—if these things really are and if we see and hear correctly, then each of them ought to be just as we thought at first, and it should not change or come to be different, but each thing always ought to be just as it is. But in fact we say that we see and hear and understand correctly.

We think that what is hot becomes cold and what is cold hot, that what is hard becomes soft and what is soft hard, and that the living dies and that it comes to be from the nonliving, and that all these things come to be different and that what was and what is now are not at all alike, but that iron, although hard, is worn away by contact with the finger, and also gold and stone and anything else that we think is enduring,[5] and that earth and stone come to be from water.

Hence these things do not agree with one another. For although we say that there are many eternal things that have definite forms and endurance, we think that all of them become different and change from what we see at any moment.

Hence it is clear that we do not see correctly and we are incorrect in thinking that those many things are. For they would not change if they were real, but each one would be just as we thought. For nothing can prevail over what is real.

But if it changes, what-is was destroyed, and what-is-not has come to be. Thus, if there are many things, they must be such as the one is.

(Simplicius, Commentary on Aristotle's
On the Heavens 558.19–559.12)

9. (B9) [That he intends what-is to be bodiless he indicated, saying:][6] Now if it is, it must be one. But being one, it must not have body. But if it had thickness, it would have parts and no longer would be one.

(Simplicius, Commentary on Aristotle's Physics 109.34–110.2)

5. Translator's note: I follow Barnes (1979/1982) in omitting the words "so that it happens that we neither see nor know the things that are," which are found in this place in the manuscripts.

6. The comment in square brackets is from Simplicius.

10. (B10) [For he himself proves that what-is is indivisible.][7]
    For if what-is is divided, it moves. But if it moved, it would
    not be.

    (Simplicius, *Commentary on Aristotle's Physics* 109.32–34)

11. (A5) Being one it is all alike. For if it were unlike, being more, it
    would no longer be one, but many.

    (Pseudo-Aristotle, *On Melissus, Xenophanes, Gorgias* 1 974a12–14)

For suggested reading, see Chapter 6, Parmenides of Elea.

7. The comment in square brackets is from Simplicius.

12. PHILOLAUS
OF CROTON

*Philolaus was born in Croton, the center of Pythagoreanism in southern
Italy. The date of his birth is controversial, and is given from anywhere
around 470 to about 430 BCE. He certainly never knew Pythagoras
himself, who died before 490. He was probably the first of the Pythagoreans
to write a book, which may have been one of Aristotle's chief sources for
his accounts of Pythagoreanism.*[1] *In Plato's* Phaedo, *two associates of
Socrates who are present at his death, Simmias and Cebes, are represented
as Pythagoreans and said to have studied with Philolaus in Thebes when
he visited mainland Greece. According to Philolaus, the cosmos is made
up of what he calls limiters and unlimiteds, fitted together in what he calls
a* harmonia *(literally a carpenter's joint; also a musical fitting together
or harmony).*[2] *A* harmonia *is expressible in a numerical ratio, and thus,
according to Philolaus, can be known. On this view, the cosmos as a series
of numerical relationships becomes intelligible to humans. In Philolaus, we
see Pythagorean assumptions about the power of number at work, although
it is possible that Aristotle's famous claim that the Pythagoreans said that
everything* is *number is Aristotle's own interpretation rather than something
any of the Pythagoreans actually said. It is not, for instance, present in any of
the extant fragments of Philolaus.*

1. **(44B1)** Nature in the *kosmos* was joined from both unlimiteds and
   limiters, and the entire *kosmos* and all the things in it.
   (Diogenes Laertius, Lives of the Philosophers 8.85)

2. **(B2)** It is necessary that the things that are be all either limiters
   or unlimited or both limiters and unlimited; but not in all cases

---

1. This is the view of Carl Huffman; Richard McKirahan is more optimistic
about Aristotle having other sources.
2. Empedocles, too, uses the term.

only unlimited.[3] Now since it is evident that they are neither from things that are all limiters nor from things that are all unlimited, it is therefore clear that both the *kosmos* and the things in it were joined together from both limiters and unlimiteds. The behavior of these things in turn makes it clear. For those of them that are from limiters limit, those that are from both limiters and unlimiteds both limit and do not limit, and those that are from unlimiteds will evidently be unlimited.

(Stobaeus, *Selections* 1.21.7a)

3. (B3) There will not be anything that is going to know at all, if all things are unlimited.

(Iamblichus, *Commentary on Nicomachus'*
Introduction to Arithmetic 7.8)

4. (B4) And in fact all the things that are known have number. For it is not possible for anything at all either to be comprehended or known without this.

(Stobaeus, *Selections* 1.21.7b)

5. (B5) In fact, number has two proper kinds, odd and even, and a third kind, even-odd from both mixed together. Of each of the two kinds there are many forms, of which each thing itself gives signs.

(Stobaeus, *Selections* 1.21.7c)

6. (B6) Concerning nature and *harmonia* this is how it is:
the being of things, which is eternal—that is, in fact, their very nature—admits knowledge that is divine and not human, except that it was impossible for any of the things that are and are known by us to have come to be if there did not exist the being of the things from which the *kosmos* is constituted—both the limiters and the unlimiteds. But since the principles are not similar or of the same kind, it would be completely impossible for them to be brought into order [or, "for them to be kept in an orderly arrangement (*kosmos*)"] if *harmonia* had not come upon them in whatever way it did. Now things that are similar and of the same kind have no need of *harmonia*, but those that are dissimilar and not of the

---

3. I follow Huffman in omitting the addition "or only limiting" (DK).

same kind or of the same speed must be connected together in *harmoniai*[4] if they are going to be kept in an orderly arrangement (*kosmos*).

(Stobaeus, *Selections* 1.21.7d)

7. (B6a) The magnitude of the *harmonia* is the fourth plus the fifth. The fifth is greater than the fourth by a 9:8 ratio. For from the lowest string to the second string is a fourth, and from the second string to the highest string is a fifth, but from the highest string to the third string is a fourth, and from the third string to the lowest string is a fifth. What is between the third string and the second string is a 9:8 ratio; the fourth has a 4:3 ratio, the fifth a 3:2 ratio, and the octave a 2:1 ratio. Thus the *harmonia* is five 9:8 ratios plus two half tones, the fifth is three 9:8 ratios plus one half-tone, and the fourth two 9:8 ratios plus one half-tone.

(Stobaeus, *Selections* 1.21.7d)

8. (B7) The first thing that was joined [harmonized], the one in the middle of the sphere, is called the hearth.

(Stobaeus, *Selections* 1.21.8)

9. (B17) The *kosmos* is one. It began to come to be right up at the middle, and from the middle <it came to be> in an upward direction in the same way as it did in a downward direction, and the things above the middle are symmetrical with those below. For, in the lower <regions> the lowest part is like the highest part <in the upper regions>, and similarly for the rest. For both <the higher and the lower> have the same relationship to the middle, unless they have been moved to another location.

(Stobaeus, *Selections* 1.15.7; based on Huffman's translation)

10. (B16) Some *logoi* are stronger than we are.

(Aristotle, *Eudemian Ethics* 2.8 1225a30; Huffman's translation)

11. (B20) [Philolaus correctly called] the number 7 motherless. [For it alone is of a nature neither to generate nor to be generated.]

(John the Lydian, *On the Months* 2.12)

---

4. Translator's note: This is the plural of *harmonia*. I accept the manuscript reading *harmoniais*.

12. (B13) The head <is the location> of intellect, the heart of soul and
sensation, the navel of the taking root and growth of the first
<part>, the genital organs of the depositing of seed and of genera-
tion. The brain contains the principle of man, the heart <contains
the principle> of animals, the navel that of plants, and the genital
organs that of them all. For they all both flourish and grow from
seed.

(Pseudo-Iamblichus, *Theological Arithmetic* 25.12)

13. (58B8) The Pythagoreans similarly posited two principles, but
added something peculiar to themselves, not that the limited and
the unlimited are distinct natures like fire or earth or something
similar, but that the unlimited itself and the one itself are the substance of what they are predicated of. This is why they call number
the substance of all things.

(Aristotle, *Metaphysics* 1.5 987a13–19)

14. (45, 3) Eurytus [late fifth century; pupil of Philolaus] assigned
what was the number of what, for example, this is the number of
a human, that is the number of a horse, like those who bring numbers into triangular and square figures, fashioning with pebbles
the forms of plants.

(Aristotle, *Metaphysics* 14.5 1092b10–13)

15. (45, 3) For example, suppose the number 250 is the definition of
human being. . . . After positing this, he [Eurytus] would take
250 pebbles, some green, some black, others red, and generally
pebbles of all colors. Then he smeared a wall with lime and drew
a human being in outline . . . and then fastened some of these pebbles in the drawn face, others in the hands, others elsewhere, and
he completed the drawing of the human being there represented
by means of pebbles equal to the units which he declared define
human being. As a result of this procedure he would state that just
as the particular sketched human being is composed of, say, 250
pebbles, so a real human being is defined by so many units.

(Alexander of Aphrodisias, *Commentary on
Aristotle's Metaphysics* 827.9–19)

16. (58B4) In numbers they [Pythagoreans] thought they observed
many resemblances to the things that are and that come to

be . . . such and such an attribute of numbers being justice, another being soul and intellect, another being decisive moment, and similarly for virtually all other things . . . since all other things seemed to be made in the likeness of numbers in their entire nature.

(Aristotle, *Metaphysics* 1.5 985b28–33)

Suggestions for Further Reading

All of these entries have further bibliographies. Complete bibliographical information for collections may be found in the bibliography in the Introduction, pp. 10–12. See also the relevant chapters in Barnes; Guthrie; McKirahan; and Kirk, Raven, and Schofield.

Burkert, W. 1972. *Lore and Science in Ancient Pythagoreanism,* translated by E. Minar. Cambridge, MA: Harvard University Press.

Dicks, D. R. 1970. *Early Greek Astronomy to Aristotle.* Ithaca: Cornell University Press.

Huffman, C. A. 2005. *Archytas of Tarentum: Pythagorean, Philosopher, and Mathematician King.* Cambridge: Cambridge University Press.

———. 2008. "Philolaus." In *The Stanford Encyclopedia of Philosophy (Fall 2008 Edition),* edited by Edward N. Zalta. http://plato.stanford.edu/archives/fall2008/entries/philolaus/.

———. 2007. "Philolaus and the Central Fire." In *Reading Ancient Texts, Volume I: Presocratics and Plato, Essays in Honour of Denis O'Brien,* edited by Suzanne Stern-Gillet and Kevin Corrigan, (eds.), pp. 57–94. Leiden: Brill.

———. 1993. *Philolaus of Croton: Pythagorean and Presocratic.* Cambridge: Cambridge University Press.

———. 2009. "The Pythagorean Conception of the Soul." In *Body and Soul in Ancient Philosophy,* edited by Dorothea Frede, pp. 21–44. Berlin: De Gruyter.

Kahn, C. 1993. "Pythagorean Philosophy before Plato," in Mourelatos, pp. 161–85.

———. 2001. *Pythagoras and the Pythagoreans.* Indianapolis: Hackett.

Mourelatos, A. P. D. 2006 "The Concept of the Universal in Some Later Pre-Platonic Cosmologists," in Gill and Pellegrin, pp. 56–76.

Mueller, I. 1997. "Greek Arithmetic, Geometry and Harmonics: Thales to Plato." In *Routledge History of Philosophy Vol. I: From the Beginning to Plato,* edited by C. C. W. Taylor, pp. 271–322. London: Routledge.

Nussbaum, Martha. 1979. "Eleatic Conventionalism and Philolaus on the Conditions of Thought." *Harvard Studies in Classical Philology* 83: pp. 63–108.

Philip, J. A. 1966. *Pythagoras and Early Pythagoreanism.* Toronto: University of Toronto Press.

Riedweg, Christoph. 2005. *Pythagoras: His Life, Teaching, and Influence.* Ithaca and London: Cornell University Press.

Schibli, H. S. 1996. "On 'The One' in Philolaus, Fragment 7." *The Classical Quarterly* n. s. 46.1: pp. 114–30.

Zhmud, L. 1989. "'All Is Number?'" *Phronesis* 34: pp. 270–92.

———. 1998. "Some Notes on Philolaus and the Pythagoreans." *Hyperboreus* 4: pp. 1–17.

13. DIOGENES OF APOLLONIA

Theophrastus says that Diogenes of Apollonia was perhaps the last of the physiologoi, *the early Greek thinkers who concentrated on theories of the natural world, the line of which began with Thales and the other Milesians. There were several Apollonias in the ancient world, and it is most likely that Diogenes came from the Apollonia on the Black Sea, which was a colony of Miletus; Anaximander was connected with its founding. The best evidence suggests that Diogenes was active after around 440 BCE; this makes him a contemporary of Melissus and probably Anaxagoras, whose theories he seems to have known. He lived at about the same time as Leucippus, although there is little evidence that he was aware of Atomism. There are references to his work in the plays of the Athenians Euripides and Aristophanes, and in Plato's* Phaedo. *Nothing certain is known of his life, although his interest in the role of the brain in perception and his studies of the veins suggest that he had an interest in medicine and was perhaps a physician as well as a physicist. Simplicius in the sixth century CE had seen a copy of Diogenes' book called* On Nature, *and Simplicius suggests that Diogenes may have written at least three other books as well. Diogenes adopts material monism: There is a single basic stuff, air, which undergoes alteration, through the mechanism of condensation and rarefaction, to become all the other elements of the cosmos; everything is a form of air. In fragment 2 (B2) he argues for monism and against metaphysical pluralism. He also argues that air is intelligent and divine. Thus, his cosmos is infused with intelligence and divinity; the degree of intelligence anything has is determined by the comparative warmth of its internal air. Diogenes wrote in prose, and his plain clear style (perhaps influenced by Anaxagoras) makes his work more accessible to students of philosophy and science than that of some of his Presocratic predecessors. Long underestimated by scholars, Diogenes is now receiving more serious attention than in the past.*

1. (64B1) In my opinion, a person beginning any discourse must present a starting point that is indisputable and an explanation [or, "style"] that is simple and serious.

(Diogenes Laertius, *Lives of the Philosophers* 9.57)[1]

2. (B2) [In *On Nature*, the only one of his works that has come into my hands, he proposes to give many proofs that in the principle he posits there is much intelligence. Immediately after the introduction he writes the following.][2] In my opinion, to sum it all up, all things that are are differentiated forms of the same thing and are the same thing. And this is manifest. For if the things that are now in this *kosmos*—earth, water, air, fire, and all the rest that are seen to exist in this *kosmos*—if any one of these were different from another, being different in its own nature, and if it were not the case that, being the same thing, it changed and was differentiated in many ways, they could not mix with each other in any way nor could help or harm come to one from another, nor could a plant grow from the earth nor an animal or anything else come to be, unless they were so constituted as to be the same thing. But all these things, being differentiated out of the same thing, come to be different things at different times and return into the same thing.

(Simplicius, *Commentary on Aristotle's Physics* 151.28–152.7)

3. (B3) [In what follows he shows that in this principle there is much intelligence.] For without intelligence it [the "same thing" in fragment 2] could not be distributed in such a way as to have the measures of all things—winter and summer, night and day, rains and winds and good weather. If anyone wants to think about the other things too, he would find that as they are arranged, they are as good as possible.

(Simplicius, *Commentary on Aristotle's Physics* 152.10–16)

1. Translator's note: Diogenes Laertius, who quotes this fragment, says that it was the beginning of Diogenes' book.
2. B2–B5 are quoted by Simplicius in his *Commentary on Aristotle's Physics* 151.28–153.17; some of Simplicius' comments are included in square brackets in the translations given here.

4. (B4) [He continues as follows, saying that men and the other animals live and have soul and intelligence from this principle, which is air.] Moreover, in addition to the preceding indications, the following, too, are important. Humans and animals live by means of air through breathing. And this [air] is both soul and intelligence for them, as will be displayed manifestly in this book. And if this departs, they die and their intelligence fails.

(Simplicius, *Commentary on Aristotle's Physics* 152.15–21)

5. (B5) [Then, a little later he continues clearly.] And in my opinion, that which possesses intelligence is what people call air, and all humans are governed by it and it rules all things. For in my opinion this very thing is god, and it reaches everything and arranges all things and is in everything. And there is no single thing that does not share in this. But no single thing shares in it in the same way as anything else, but there are many forms both of air itself and of intelligence. For it is multiform—hotter and colder, drier and wetter, more stable and possessing a sharper movement, and unlimitedly many other alterations are in it, both of flavor and of color. And the soul of all animals is the same thing, air hotter than the air outside in which we are located, but much colder than the air near the sun. This heat is not identical in any two animals, since it is not identical even in any two humans, but it differs—not greatly, but so that they are similar. Moreover, it is impossible for any of the things that are being differentiated to be exactly like one another without becoming the same thing. Now since the differentiation is multiform, also the animals are multiform and many and are like one another in neither shape nor way of life nor intelligence, on account of the large number of their differentiations. Nevertheless, all things live, see, and hear by means of the same thing, and all get the rest of their intelligence from the same thing.

(Simplicius, *Commentary on Aristotle's Physics* 152.21–153.13)

6. (B6) [And next he shows that the sperm of animals has the form of air, and thoughts come into being when air occupies the whole body through the veins, together with blood. In the course of this discussion he gives an accurate anatomy of the veins. In these

words he is clearly seen to say that the principle is what people call air.]³

This is an account of the blood vessels in humans. There are two very large ones. These run through the belly alongside the backbone, one on the right side and one on the left. Each goes toward the leg on the same side, and up toward the head alongside the collar bone through the throat. From these, blood vessels extend through the entire body, from the vessel on the right to the parts on the right, and from the vessel on the left to the parts on the left. The largest two go next to the backbone to the heart, and others, a little higher up, go through the chest under the armpit to the hand on the same side. One of them is called the splenetic vessel, the other the hepatic. Each of them is divided at the extremity, one part going to the thumb, the other to the palm, and from these, tiny vessels with many branches go to the rest of the hand and to the fingers. Other tinier vessels extend from the first vessels—from the one on the right side, to the liver, from the one on the left side, to the spleen and kidneys. The vessels that go to the legs branch at the junction of the legs and run through the entire length of the thigh and are visibly thick. Another one runs inside the thigh and is smaller and less thick than the other. Then they go next to the knee, to the shin and the foot in the same way as the ones that go to the hands, and they arrive at the sole of the foot, and from there they divide and go to the toes. Many tiny vessels branch off from them in the belly and ribs. Some go to the head through the throat and are visibly large in the neck. Many others branch off from the end of each of them and go to the head, some crossing from the right side to the left, and others from the left side to the right. They end at each ear. On each side there is another vessel in the neck next to the large vessel, a little smaller than it, to which most of the vessels that come from the head are connected. These too go through the throat on the inside, and from each of them others go under the shoulder blade to the hands, and they are visible next to the splenetic and hepatic vessels and other vessels that are a little smaller. These are the ones that [physicians] lance when there is pain under the skin. If there is pain in the region of the belly, they lance the hepatic and the splenetic vessels. Others begin

3. Editor's note: This introductory passage is from Simplicius, *Commentary on Aristotle's Physics* 153.13–17.

from these and go to the breasts. There are others, tiny ones, that go from each of these through the spinal marrow to the testicles. Others go under the skin, through the flesh, to the kidneys and end at the testicles in men and in women at the uterus. The vessels from the belly are at first wider, and then they become narrower until they cross from right to left and from left to right. These are called the spermatic vessels. The thickest blood is absorbed by the fleshy parts of the body; the excess goes to these regions [the genital organs] and becomes thin, hot, and foamy.

(Aristotle, *History of Animals* 3.2 511b30–512b11)

7. (B7) And this very thing [air] is an eternal and immortal body, and by means of it some things come to be and others pass away.

(Simplicius, *Commentary on Aristotle's Physics* 153.19–20)

8. (B8) But this seems clear to me, that it [air] is large and strong and eternal and immortal and knowing many things.

(Simplicius, *Commentary on Aristotle's Physics* 153.20–21)

9. (A1) Air is the element. There are infinite *kosmoi* and infinite void. The air, by being condensed and rarefied, is generative of the *kosmoi*. Nothing comes to be from or perishes into what-is-not. The earth is round and is supported in the center [of the *kosmos*] and has undergone its process of formation through the rotation resulting from the hot and the solidification caused by the cold.

(Diogenes Laertius, *Lives of the Philosophers* 9.57)

10. (A6) All things are in motion and there are infinite *kosmoi*. His account of cosmogony is the following: The whole is in motion and comes to be rare in one place, dense in another. Where the dense part chanced to come together it formed the earth by revolving, and the other things in the same way. The lightest things occupied the highest location and produced the sun.

(Pseudo-Plutarch, *Miscellanies* 12)

11. (A19) Diogenes attributes the senses, as well as life and thought, to air. . . . The sense of smell is due to the air around the brain. . . . Hearing occurs when the air in the ears is set in motion by the air outside and is passed on toward the brain. Sight occurs when things are reflected in the pupil, and the reflection, being mixed

with the air inside, produces sensation. Evidence of this is the fact that if the veins [in the eyes] become inflamed, it [the reflection?] is not mixed with the air inside and we do not see, although the reflection is there just the same. Taste occurs in the tongue because of its rare and soft nature. Concerning touch he declared nothing, neither its functioning nor its objects. . . . The interior air, which is a small part of god, is what perceives. Evidence of this is that often when we have our mind on other matters we neither see nor hear. Pleasure and pain arise in the following manner: pleasure whenever a large amount of air is mixed with the blood and makes it light, being in accordance with its nature and penetrating the whole body; and pain whenever the air is contrary to its nature and is not mixed, and the blood coagulates and becomes weaker and denser. Similarly also boldness and health and the opposites. . . . Thought, as was said, is due to air that is pure and dry. For moisture hinders the mind. For this reason thought is diminished when we are asleep, drunk, or full. . . . This is why children are foolish. . . . They are also prone to anger and in general easily roused and changeable because air, which is great in quantity, is separated by small intervals. This is also the cause of forgetfulness: When the air does not go through the entire body, people cannot comprehend.

(Theophrastus, *On Sensation* 39–45)

Suggestions for Further Reading

All of these entries have further bibliographies. Complete bibliographical information for collections may be found in the bibliography in the Introduction, pp. 10–12. See also the relevant chapters in Barnes; Guthrie; McKirahan; and Kirk, Raven, and Schofield.

Crivellato E., F. Mallardi, and D. Ribatti. 2006. "Diogenes of Apollonia: A Pioneer in Vascular Anatomy." *Anatomical Record—Part B: New Anatomist* 289/4: pp. 116–20.

Graham, D. W. 2006. *Explaining the Cosmos.* Chapter 10, "Diogenes of Apollonia and Material Monism," pp. 277–93. Princeton: Princeton University Press.

Laks, A. 2008. *Diogène d'Apollonie: Edition, traduction et commentaire des fragments et témoignages.* Sankt Augustin: Academia Verlag.

———. "Speculating about Diogenes of Apollonia," in Curd and Graham, pp. 353–64.

14. THE SOPHISTS

From the time of Homer onward Greek writers were concerned with questions about the best way of life for a human being and just what virtues or excellences a good person needed to cultivate. Herodotus and other early historians had also provided information about other cultures and their social and political systems and compared these with the Greeks. Yet it was primarily in the fifth century BCE that theories about moral, political, and social questions began to be developed. It was primarily the Sophists who raised and discussed these issues, although as we have seen, some of the Presocratic philosophers were also participants in these debates. Most of the Sophists were professional teachers and rhetoricians, but some active politicians in Athens came to be considered Sophists, and although they did not form a single school or group, there were enough similarities in their activities and viewpoints for them to be considered together. The word "sophist" has its roots in sophos meaning "wise," and, in its earliest uses, someone who was a sophistēs was a master in his craft or an expert. In general, the Sophists can be considered as practitioners and teachers of wisdom. This obviously raises the question, "What is wisdom?" and the Sophists aimed to answer that question, as well as questions about the other excellences or virtues needed by a successful citizen of a Greek city-state, or polis. Travelling throughout Greece, teaching, giving rhetorical displays, and competing with one another for paying students and audiences, the Sophists were a major part of social and intellectual life, for the questions they raised were fundamental to life in a Greek polis.

Our information about the Sophists comes mainly from Plato, who was not an impartial witness. Like Socrates, his intellectual hero, Plato was suspicious of sophistic teaching and claims to knowledge, and was scandalized by the fact that the Sophists charged for their teaching and would take on any pupil who could afford the price. Many of Plato's dialogues show Socrates demonstrating that one Sophist or another fails to understand his own views or the nature of the wisdom that the Sophist purports to teach. In his writings, Plato explicitly contrasts Socrates, the independent lover of wisdom (the philosophos) with the mere expert technician (the sophistēs) *who pleases crowds rather than searching seriously for the truth. We should be wary of accepting Plato's views uncritically, and we should treat his evidence about the Sophists—in such dialogues as* Protagoras, Gorgias, *and the two named after Hippias—with great care.*

The Sophists included here are representative of the movement and its methods; there are short claims illustrating views about knowledge and some longer speeches. The texts given here show that a sharp distinction between the philosophers and the Sophists may be untenable.

14.1. Protagoras

Protagoras was perhaps the most famous of the early Sophists. He was born in Abdera (home of Democritus as well) around 490 BCE and died about 420. He was often in Athens and part of the circle around Pericles (one wonders if he knew Anaxagoras), but he was also very well known in the western Greek cities of Sicily and Southern Italy. Plato's dialogue Protagoras *presents an unforgettable (if perhaps not entirely trustworthy) picture of the excitement that Protagoras could generate.*

1. (80A5) [Protagoras on what he teaches and the value of his teachings.] My boy, if you associate with me, the result will be that the very day you begin you will return home a better person, and the same will happen the next day too. Each day you will make constant progress toward being better. . . . [Protagoras teaches a young man] Good counsel concerning his personal affairs, so that he may best manage his own household, and also concerning the city's affairs, so that as far as the city's affairs go he may be most powerful in acting and in speaking.

   (Plato, *Protagoras* 318a, 318e–319a)

2. (80B3) Teaching requires nature and training. . . . Learning must begin at an early age.

   (*Anecdota Parisiensia* I 171, 31)

3. (80B10) Art (*tekhnē*) without practice and practice without art are nothing.

   (Stobaeus, *Selections* 3.29.80)

4. (80B11) Education is not implanted in the soul unless one reaches a greater depth.

(Pseudo-Plutarch, *On Training* 178.25)

5. (80B4) Concerning the gods I am unable to know either that they are or that they are not or what their appearance is like. For many are the things that hinder knowledge: the obscurity of the matter and the shortness of human life.

(Eusebius, *Preparation of the Gospel* 14.3.7)

6. (80B7) [It is not true that geometry studies perceptible magnitudes . . .] For perceptible lines are not the kind of things the geometer talks about, since no perceptible thing is straight or curved in that way, nor is a circle tangent to a ruler at a point, but the way Protagoras used to say in refuting the geometers.

(Aristotle, *Metaphysics* 3.2 997b34–998a4)

7. Protagoras says of mathematics, the subject matter is unknowable and the terminology distasteful.

(Philodemus of Gadara, *On Poetry* P.Herc. 1676, col. 1.12–13; not in DK)

8. (80B1) A person is the measure of all things—of things that are, that they are, and of things that are not, that they are not.

(Sextus Empiricus, *Against the Mathematicians* 7.60)

9. (80A1) He was the first to use in dialectic the argument of Antisthenes that attempts to prove that contradiction is impossible.

(Diogenes Laertius, *Lives of the Philosophers* 9.53)

10. (80A1) Protagoras was the first to declare that there are two mutually opposed arguments on any subject.

(Diogenes Laertius, *Lives of the Philosophers* 9.51)

11. (80A21) Protagoras made the weaker and stronger argument and taught his students to blame and praise the same person.

(Stephanus of Byzantium, s.v. *Abdera*)

12. (80A21) [Aristotle on Protagoras' method.] This is making the weaker argument stronger. And people were rightly annoyed at Protagoras' promise.

(Aristotle, *Rhetoric* 2.24 1402a24–26)

What follows is an extract from the anonymous Dissoi Logoi (Twofold Arguments *or* Contrasting Arguments), *a sample collection of arguments for and against various claims, such as for and against Good and Bad, Truth and Falsity, Just and Unjust, and so on. It gives a sample of the sorts of arguments Protagoras or another Sophist might give.*

13. (90, 4) (1) Twofold arguments are also stated concerning the false and the true, of which one declares that true *logos* [speech, statement] and false *logos* are different from one another, and others that they are the same. (2) And I say the following. First, that true and false *logos* are expressed in the same words. Second, when a *logos* is spoken, if events have occurred the way the *logos* is spoken, the *logos* is true, but if they have not occurred, the same *logos* is false. (3) Suppose it accuses someone of sacrilege. If the deed took place, the *logos* is true, but if it did not take place, it is false. And the *logos* of the defendant is the same. And the courts judge the same *logos* to be both false and true. (4) Next, if we are seated one next to the other, and we [each] say "I am an initiate of the mysteries," we will all say the same thing, but only I will be truthful, since in fact I am <the only> one <who is>. (5) Now it is obvious that the same *logos* is false whenever falsehood is present to it and true whenever truth is, in the same way a person is the same individual as a boy and as a youth and as an adult and as an old man. (6) It is also stated that false *logos* and true *logos* are different from one another, differing in name just as they differ in fact. For if anyone asks those who say that the same *logos* is both false and true which of the two [namely, false and true] the *logos* that they are stating is, then if it is false, clearly they [the true *logos* and the false *logos*] are two [and therefore not the same]. But if it is true, this same *logos* is also false. And if anyone has ever spoken or borne witness of things that are true, it follows that these same things are false. And if he knows any man to be true, also he knows the same man to be

false. (7) As a result of the argument they say these things because
if the thing occurred the *logos* is true, but if it did not then it is false.
Therefore it is not their name that differs, but the fact of the matter.
(8) Moreover, if anyone should ask the jurors what they are judging
(since they are not present at the events), (9) these people too agree
that the *logos* with which falsehood is mixed is false, and that with
which truth is mixed is true. This is the entire difference.

(Dissoi Logoi 90.4)

14.2. Gorgias

*Gorgias of Leontini in Sicily was a contemporary of Protagoras and was
also born around 490 BCE; there are reports that he was well over 100 years
old when he died. As well-known as Protagoras, Gorgias described himself
as a teacher of rhetoric, and it appears that his formal and elaborate writing
style was influential. He came to Athens on a diplomatic mission in 427
and was famous for his speeches, which he would give in public displays,
some of which survive, and two of which are included below. One, a defense
of Helen of Troy, explores the power of persuasion through rhetoric. The
other, a fascinating response to (or parody of?) Eleatic metaphysics is called*
On Nature, or, On What Is Not. *This essay, written in the 440s and so
contemporary with Melissus, influenced later philosophers, including Plato,
and so it is given in full here.*

14. (82B11) *Praise of Helen* [in part]
(5) I will set forth the reasons for which it was likely that Helen's
voyage to Troy took place. (6) She did what she did through the
will of Fate and the designs of the gods and decrees of Necessity
or because she was taken by force, persuaded by words (*logoi*), or
conquered by Love. . . . (8) Not even if speech (*logos*) persuaded
and deceived her soul, is it hard to make a defense against this
charge and free her from blame, as follows. *Logos* is a powerful
master, which by means of the smallest and most invisible body
accomplishes most divine deeds. For it can put an end to fear,
remove grief, instill joy, and increase pity. I will prove how this
is so. (9) But it is to the opinion of my audience that I must prove
it. I both consider and define all poetry to be speech (*logos*) with
meter. Those who hear it are overcome with fearful shuddering,

tearful pity, and mournful yearning, and over the good fortunes and ill-farings of other people and their affairs the soul experiences a feeling of its own, through the words (*logoi*). Come now, let me shift from one argument (*logos*) to another. (10) Inspired incantations bring on pleasure and bring away grief through words (*logoi*). For conversing with the soul's opinion the power of incantation charms, persuades, and changes it by witchcraft. Two arts of witchcraft and magic have been discovered—errors of the soul and deceptions of opinion. (11) All who have persuaded or who persuade anyone of anything do so by fashioning false *logos*. For if on all subjects everyone had memory of the past, <a conception> of the present, and foreknowledge of the future, *logos* would not be similarly similar as it is for people who, as things are, cannot easily remember the past, consider the present, or divine the future. Thus, on most matters, most people make opinion an adviser to their soul. But opinion is fallible and uncertain and involves those who make use of it in fallible and uncertain successes. (12) What, then, keeps us from supposing that Helen too, against her will, came under the influence of *logoi* just as if she had been taken by the force of mighty men? For it was possible to see how persuasion prevails, which lacks the appearance of necessity but has the same power.[1] For *logos*, which persuaded, compelled the soul, which it persuaded, both to believe what was said and to approve what was done. Therefore, the one who persuaded, since he compelled, is unjust, and the one who was persuaded, since she was compelled by *logos,* is wrongly blamed. (13) As to the fact that persuasion added to *logos* makes whatever impression it likes on the soul, one should attend first to the accounts (*logoi*) of the astronomers, who replace one opinion with another and so make things incredible and unclear seem apparent to the eyes of opinion; second, to compulsory competitions that use speeches (*logoi*) in which a single *logos* written with art (*tekhnē*) but not spoken with truth delights and persuades a large crowd; and third, to contests of philosophers' accounts (*logoi*), in which is revealed how easily the swiftness of thought makes our confidence in our opinion change. (14) The power of *logos* has the same relation (*logos*) to the order of the soul as the order of drugs has to the nature of bodies.

---

1. Translator's note: The text of this sentence is corrupt. I follow Diels' suggestions (DK vol. 2, p. 291).

For as different drugs expel different humors from the body, and some put an end to sickness and others to life, so some *logoi* cause grief, others joy, some fear, others render their hearers bold, and still others drug and bewitch the soul through an evil persuasion. (15) It has been stated that if she was persuaded by *logos* she did not do wrong but was unfortunate. . . . (21) By my account (*logos*) I have removed ill fame from a woman. I have stayed faithful to the rule (*nomos*) I stipulated at the beginning of my *logos*. I have attempted to put an end to the injustice of blame and the ignorance of opinion. I wanted to write the *logos* as a praise of Helen and an entertainment for myself.

15. (82B3)[2] *On What Is Not or On Nature*
(66) He concludes as follows that nothing is: if \<something\> is, either what-is is or what-is-not \<is\>, or both what-is and what-is-not \<are\>. But it is the case neither that what-is is, as he will show, nor that what-is-not is, as he will justify, nor that both what-is and what-is-not are, as he will teach this too. Therefore, it is not the case that anything is.

(67) And in fact, what-is-not is not. For if what-is-not is, it will be and not be at the same time. For in that it is considered as not being, it will not be, but in that it *is* not being, on the other hand, it will be. But it is completely absurd for something to be and not be at the same time. Therefore, it is not the case that what-is-not is.

And differently: if what-is-not is, what-is will not be, since they are opposites, and if being is an attribute of what-is-not, not-being will be an attribute of what-is. But it is certainly not the case that what what-is is not, and so neither will what-is-not be.

(68) Further, neither is it the case that what-is is. For if what-is is, it is either eternal or generated or eternal and generated at the same time. But it is neither eternal nor generated nor both, as we will show. Therefore it is not the case that what-is is. For if what-is is eternal (we must begin at this point), it does not have any beginning. (69) For everything that comes to be has some beginning, but what is eternal, being ungenerated did not have a beginning. But if

2. Translator's note: This is a translation of the version in Sextus Empiricus, *Against the Mathematicians* 7.65–86 = DK 82B3. The shorter summary in pseudo–Aristotle, *On Melissus, Xenophanes, and Gorgias,* Chs. 5–6 (not in DK), is preferable at some points.

it does not have a beginning it is unlimited, and if it is unlimited it is nowhere. For if it is anywhere, that in which it is is different from it, and so what-is will no longer be unlimited, since it is enclosed in something. For what encloses is larger than what is enclosed, but nothing is larger than what is unlimited, and so what is unlimited is not anywhere. (70) Further, it is not enclosed in itself, either. For "that in which" and "that in it" will be the same, and what-is will become two, place and body (for "that in which" is place, and "that in it" is body). But this is absurd, so what-is is not in itself, either. And so, if what-is is eternal it is unlimited, but if it is unlimited it is nowhere, and if it is nowhere it is not. So if what-is is eternal, it is not at all.

(71) Further, what-is cannot be generated either. For if it has come to be it did so either from a thing that is or from a thing that is not. But it has come to be neither from what-is (for if it is a thing that is, it has not come to be, but already is), nor from what-is-not (for what-is-not cannot generate anything, since what generates anything must of necessity share in existence). Therefore it is not the case that what-is is generated either. (72) In the same ways, it is not both eternal and generated at the same time. For these exclude one another, and if what-is is eternal it has not come to be, and if it has come to be it is not eternal. So if what-is is neither eternal nor generated nor both together, what-is would not be.

(73) And differently, if it is, it is either one or many. But it is neither one nor many, as will be shown. Therefore it is not the case that what-is is. For if it is one, it is either a quantity or continuous or a magnitude or a body. But whichever of these it is, it is not one, but being a quantity, it will be divided, and if it is continuous it will be cut. Similarly if conceived as a magnitude it will not be indivis- ible. And if it chances to be a body, it will be three-dimensional, for it will have length, width, and depth. But it is absurd to say that what-is is none of these. Therefore it is not the case that what-is is one. (74) Further, it is not many. For if it is not one it is not many either. For the many is a compound of individual ones, and so since <the thesis that what-is is> one is refuted, <the thesis that what-is is> many is refuted along with it. But it is altogether clear from this that neither what-is nor what-is-not is.

(75) It is easy to conclude that neither is it the case that both of them are, what-is and what-is-not. For if what-is-not is and what-is is, then what-is-not will be the same as what-is as regards being.

And for this reason neither of them is. For it is agreed that what-is-not is not, and what-is has been shown to be the same as this. So it too will not be. (76) However, if what-is is the same as what-is-not, it is not possible for both to be. For if both <are>, then they are not the same, and if <they are> the same, then <it is> not <the case that> both <are>. It follows that nothing is. For if neither what-is is nor what-is-not nor both, and nothing aside from these is conceived of, nothing is.

(77) Next in order is to teach that even if something is, it is unknowable and inconceivable by humans. For if things that are thought of, says Gorgias, are not things-that-are, what-is is not thought of. And reasonably so. For just as if things that are thought of have the attribute of being white, being thought of would be an attribute of white things, so if things that are thought of have the attribute of not being things-that-are, not to be thought of will necessarily be an attribute of things-that-are. (78) This is why the claim that if things that are thought of are not things-that-are, then what-is is not thought of is sound and preserves the sequence of argument. But things that are thought of (for we must assume this) are not things-that-are, as we will show. Therefore it is not the case that what-is is thought of. Further, it is completely clear that things that are thought of are not things-that-are. (79) For if things that are thought of are things-that-are, all things that are thought of are—indeed, however anyone thinks of them. But this is apparently false. For if someone thinks of a person flying or chariots racing in the sea, it is not the case that forthwith a person is flying or chariots racing in the sea. And so, it is not the case that things that are thought of are things-that-are. (80) In addition, if things that are thought of are things-that-are, things-that-are-not will not be thought of. For opposites have opposite attributes, and what-is-not is opposite to what-is. For this reason, if being thought of is an attribute of what-is, not being thought of will assuredly be an attribute of what-is-not. But this is absurd. For Scylla and Chimaera and many things-that-are-not are thought of. Therefore it is not the case that what-is is thought of. (81) And just as things that are seen are called visible because they are seen and things that are heard are called audible because they are heard, and we do not reject visible things because they are not heard or dismiss audible things because they are not seen (for each ought to be judged by its own sense, not by another), so also things that are

thought of will be, even if they may not be seen by vision or heard by hearing, because they are grasped by their own criterion. (82) So if someone thinks that chariots race in the sea, even if he does not see them, he ought to believe that there are chariots racing in the sea. But this is absurd. Therefore it is not the case that what-is is thought of and comprehended.

(83) But even if it should be comprehended it cannot be expressed to another. For if things-that-are are visible and audible and generally perceptible and in fact are external objects, and of these the visible are comprehended by vision and the audible by hearing and not vice versa, how can these be communicated to another? (84) For that by which we communicate is *logos*, but *logos* is not the objects, the things-that-are. Therefore it is not the case that we communicate things-that-are to our neighbors, but *logos*, which is different from the objects. So just as the visible could not become audible and vice versa, thus, since what-is is an external object, it could not become our *logos*. (85) But if it were not *logos*, it would not have been revealed to another. In fact, *logos*, he says, is composed from external things, that is, perceptible things, falling upon us. For from encountering flavor there arises in us the *logos* that is expressed with reference to this quality, and from the incidence on the senses of color arises the *logos* with reference to color. But if so, it is not the *logos* that makes manifest the external <object>, but the external <object> that comes to be communicative of the *logos*. (86) Further, it is not possible to say that *logos* is an object in the way visible and audible things are, so that objects that are can be communicated by it, which is an object that is. For, he says, even if *logos* is an object, it anyway differs from all other objects, and visible bodies differ most from *logos*. For the visible is grasped by one organ, *logos* by another. Therefore it is not the case that *logos* makes manifest the great number of objects, just as they do not reveal the nature of one another.

(Sextus Empiricus, *Against the Mathematicians* 7.65–86)

14.3. Prodicus

Prodicus was born on Ceos, an Aegean island near Attica, around 460 BCE, and probably lived into the fourth century. Growing wealthy from his teaching and speech-giving, he was well-traveled and was an acquaintance of Socrates (in some Platonic dialogues Socrates says that he had been a student

*of Prodicus; there is disagreement about how seriously to take this claim).
Surviving fragments indicate that Prodicus was interested in rhetoric and
logic, ethics and virtue, and the origins of religion: he was said to have denied
the reality of the gods.*

16. There is a reference to the paradoxical view of Prodicus that contra-
    diction is impossible. What does this mean? It goes against every-
    one's judgment and opinion. For in both practical and intellectual
    matters we are constantly conversing with people who contradict
    us. He says dogmatically that contradiction is impossible, because
    if two people contradict one another they are both speaking, but
    they cannot both be speaking with reference to the same fact. He
    says that only the one who speaks the truth is reporting the fact
    as it is, while the person who contradicts him does not state the
    fact.

    (Didymus the Blind, *Commentary on Ecclesiastes*; not in DK)

17. (84B5) The ancients believed that the sun and moon, rivers and
    springs, and in general everything that benefits our life were gods
    because of the benefit deriving from them.

    (Sextus Empiricus, *Against the Mathematicians* 9.18)

18. He says that the gods worshipped by men neither exist nor have
    knowledge, but that the ancients exalted crops and everything else
    that is useful for life.

    (P.Herc. 1428 col. 19.12–19; not in DK)

14.4. Hippias

*Hippias was born in Elis, near Olympia in the Peloponnese; his birth
date is unknown, but he was still living in the year of Socrates' death. He
was another wealthy and successful Sophist. Plato makes fun of him as a
polymath who can even make his own shoes, and presents him as rather
dim-witted, but this is clearly a caricature. Hippias taught rhetoric, including
mnemonics, and was interested in mathematics and geometry, where he
made an important discovery, as well as in the arts. He was famous both for
his rhetorical displays, many given at Olympia during the games, and for
his "improvisational sophistry"—making speeches on any subject proposed*

by a member of his audience. He was also an early historian, compiling a list of Olympic victors, and most significantly, he collected texts of poets and philosophers, thus beginning the tradition of the history of philosophy.

19. (86B6) Some of these things may have been said by Orpheus, some by Musaeus—in short, in different places by different authors— some by Hesiod, Homer, or other poets, and some in prose works by Greeks or foreigners. From all of them I [Hippias] have collected the most important ones that are related, and I will compose out of them this original and multiform account.

(Clement of Alexandria, *Miscellanies* 6.2.15)

20. How can anyone suppose that laws are a serious matter or believe in them, since it often happens that the very people who make them repeal them and substitute and pass others in their place?[3]

(Xenophon, *Memorabilia* 4.4.14; not in DK)

14.5. Antiphon

The Sophist we know as Antiphon is probably Antiphon of Rhamnous. He was thus a native of Attica and a citizen of Athens and so was eligible to hold political office in Athens. Born around 480 BCE, he had wide philosophical and scientific interests, but it is for his views on justice that he is best known. Here he considers the relation between nature (phusis) *and law or customs* (nomos, *pl.* nomoi).

21. (87A44a) (1) Justice is a matter of not transgressing what the *nomoi* prescribe in whatever city one is a citizen. A person would make most advantage of justice for himself if he treated the *nomoi* as important in the presence of witnesses and treated the decrees of *phusis* as important when alone and with no witnesses present. For the decrees of *nomoi* are extra additions, those of *phusis* are necessary; those of the *nomoi* are the products of agreement, not of

3. Translator's note: This passage occurs in conversation with Socrates in a work by Xenophon. How closely it reflects the actual views of Hippias is impossible to say.

natural growth, whereas those of *phusis* are the products of natural growth, not of agreement. (2) If those who made the agreement do not notice a person transgressing the prescriptions of *nomoi*, he is free from both disgrace and penalty, but not so if they do notice him. But if, contrary to possibility, anyone violates any of the things that are innate by *phusis*, the harm is no less if no one notices and no greater if all observe. For he does not suffer harm as a result of opinion but as a result of truth. . . .

This is the entire purpose of considering these matters—that most of the things that are just according to *nomos* are established in a way that is hostile to *phusis*. For *nomoi* have been established for the eyes as to what they must (3) see and what they must not, and for the ears as to what they must hear and what they must not, and for the tongue as to what it must say and what it must not, and for the hands as to what they must do and what they must not, and for the feet as to where they must go and where they must not, and for the mind as to what it must desire and what it must not. Now the things from which the *nomoi* deter humans are no more in accord with or suited to *phusis* than the things that they promote.

Living and dying are matters of *phusis*, and living results for them from what is advantageous, dying from what is not advantageous. (4) But the advantages that are established by the *nomoi* are bonds on *phusis*, and those established by *phusis* are free.

And so things that cause pain, at least when thought of correctly, do not help *phusis* more than things that give pleasure. Therefore it will not be painful things that are advantageous rather than pleasant things. For things that are truly advantageous must not cause harm but benefit. Now the things that are advantageous by *phusis* are among these. . . .

<But according to *nomos*, those are correct> who defend themselves after suffering (5) and are not first to do wrong, and those who do good to parents who are bad to them, and who permit others to accuse them on oath but do not themselves accuse on oath. You will find many of these cases hostile to *phusis*. They permit people to suffer more pain when less is possible and to have less pleasure when more is possible and to receive injury when it is not necessary.

Now if some assistance came from the *nomoi* for those who submitted to these conditions and some damage to those who do not submit but resist, (6) obedience to the *nomoi* would not be unhelpful. But as things are, it is obvious that the justice that stems from *nomos* is insufficient to aid those who submit. In the first place, it permits the one who suffers to suffer and the wrongdoer to do wrong, and it was not at the time of the wrongdoing able to prevent either the sufferer from suffering or the wrongdoer from doing wrong. And when the case is brought to trial for punishment, there is no special advantage for the one who has suffered over the wrongdoer. For he must persuade the jury that he suffered and that he is able to exact the penalty. And it is open to the wrongdoer to deny it. . . . (7) However convincing the accusation is on behalf of the accuser, the defense can be just as convincing. For victory comes through speech.[4]

(Oxyrhynchus Papyrus XI no. 1364, col. 1, line 6 to col. 7, line 15)

As the passage from Antiphon shows, the question of whether law and morality are grounded in nature or convention was a major subject of debate. Here are two texts that explore that question, the first from Critias, an aristocratic Athenian (related to Plato) and an associate of Socrates, who became one of the Thirty Tyrants after the defeat of Athens by Sparta in 404 BCE. Critias defends nomos *as the source of civilization. Finally, there is a late (for the Presocratic period) anonymous text called the* Anonymus Iamblichi *(usually dated to about 400), which argues that* nomos *is grounded in* phusis.

22. (88B25 lines 1–8) *Critias on nomos*
There was a time when human life was without order,
on the level of beasts, and subject to force;
when there was no reward for the good
or punishment for the bad.
And then, I think, humans established
nomoi as punishers, so that justice would be the mighty ruler
of all equally and would have violence (*hubris*) as its slave,
and anyone who did wrong would be punished.

(Sextus Empiricus, *Against the Mathematicians* 9.54)

4. Translator's note: The last part of the text is uncertain.

23. (DK89,6 and 7) Selections from *The Anonymous Iamblichi*

(6.1) No one should set out to maximize his own advantage or suppose that power used for one's advantage is *aretē* [virtue] and obedience to *nomoi* is cowardice. This is the most wicked thought, and it results in everything diametrically opposed to what is good: evil and harm. For if humans were by *phusis* unable to live singly but yielding to necessity came together to live with one another and discovered all their life and their contrivances for living, but it is impossible for them to live with one another and to conduct their lives in the absence of *nomoi* (since that way they would suffer more damage than they would by living alone)—on account of these necessities *nomos* and justice are kings among humans, and in no way can they depart. For they are firmly bound into our *phusis*.

(6.2) If, then, someone were born who had from the beginning the following sort of *phusis*: invulnerable in his flesh, not subject to disease, without feelings, superhuman, and hard as steel in body and soul—perhaps one might have thought that power used for personal advantage would be sufficient for such a person, since such a person could be scot-free even if he did not subject himself to the law (*nomos*). But this person does not think correctly. (6.3) Even if there were such a person, though there could not be, he would survive by being an ally of the laws (*nomoi*) and of justice, strengthening them and using his might for them and for what assists them, but otherwise he could not last. (6.4) For it would seem that all people would become enemies of a person with such a nature [*phunti*, related to *phusis*], and through their own observance of *nomos* and their numbers they would overcome him by craft or force and would prevail. (6.5) So it is obvious that power itself—real power—is preserved through *nomos* and justice.

(7)[5] It is worthwhile to learn these facts about *eunomia* and *anomia*—how big the difference is between them, and that *eunomia* is the best thing both for the community and for the individual, and *anomia* is the worst, for the greatest harm arises immediately from *anomia*. Let us begin by indicating first what results from *eunomia*.

---

5. Translator's note: Here the *Anonymus Iamblichi* contrasts *eunomia* (a condition where the *nomoi* are good and people abide by them) and *anomia* (the opposite of *eunomia*), which the author seems to conceive as a condition in which each person pursues his or her own advantage in competition with others.

(7.1) In the first place, trust arises from *eunomia,* and this benefits all people greatly and is one of the great goods. For as a result of it, money becomes available, and so even if there is little it is sufficient, since it is in circulation, but without it not even a great deal of money would be enough. (7.2) Fortunes and misfortunes in money and life are managed most suitably for people as a result of *eunomia.* For those enjoying good fortune can use it in safety and without danger of plots, while those suffering ill fortune are aided by the fortunate through their mutual dealings and trust, which result from *eunomia.* (7.3) Through *eunomia,* moreover, the time people devote to *pragmata* [a word that can mean "government," "public business," or "troubles"] is idle, but that devoted to the activities of life is productive. (7.4) In *eunomia* people are free from the most unpleasant concern and engage in the most pleasant, since concern about *pragmata* is most unpleasant and concern about one's activities is most pleasant. (7.5) Also when they go to sleep, which is a rest from troubles for people, they go to it without fear and unworried about painful matters, and when they rise from it they have other similar experiences and do not suddenly become fearful. Nor after this very pleasant change [that is, sleep] do they expect the day to bring poverty but they look forward to it without fear directing their concern without grief toward the activities of life, lightening their labors with trust and confident hopes that they will get good things as a result. For all these things *eunomia* is responsible.

(7.6) And war, which is the source of the greatest evils for people, leading as it does to destruction and slavery—this too comes more to those who practice *anomia,* less to those practicing *eunomia.* (7.7) There are many other goods found in *eunomia* that assist life, and also from it comes consolation for our difficulties. These are the evils that come from *anomia.* (7.8) In the first place, people do not have time for their activities and are engaged in the most unpleasant thing—*pragmata,* not activities—and because of mistrust and lack of mutual dealings they hoard money and do not make it available, so it becomes rare even if there is much. (7.9) Ill fortune and good fortune minister to the opposite results [from what occurs under *eunomia*]: good fortune is not safe in *anomia* but is plotted against, and bad fortune is not driven off but is strengthened through mistrust and the absence of mutual dealings. (7.10) War from outside is more frequently brought against a land, and domestic faction comes from the same cause, and if it did not occur earlier it happens then. Also it happens that people are always involved in *pragmata* because of plots that come from one another, which force them to live constantly on guard and to make counterplots against each other. (7.11) When they are awake their thoughts are not pleasant, and when they go to sleep their receptacle [that is, sleep] is not pleasant but full of fear, and their awakening is fearful and frightening and leads a person to sudden memories of his troubles. These and all the previously mentioned evils result from *anomia*.

(7.12) Also tyranny, so great and so foul an evil, arises from nothing else but *anomia*. Some people suppose—all who do not understand correctly—that a tyrant comes from some other source, and that people are deprived of their freedom without being themselves responsible but compelled by the tyrant when he has been established. But they do not consider this correctly. (7.13) For whoever thinks that a king or a tyrant arises from anything else than *anomia* and personal advantage is an idiot. For when everyone turns to evil, this is what happens. For it is impossible for humans to live without *nomoi* and justice. (7.14) So when these two things—*nomos* and justice—are missing from the mass of the people, that is exactly when the guardianship and protection of them passes to a single person. How else could solitary rule be transferred to a single person unless the *nomos* had been driven out that benefited the mass of the people? (7.15) For this man who is going to destroy justice and abolish *nomos*, which is common and advantageous to all, must be made of steel if he intends to strip these things from the mass of the people, he being one and they many. (7.16) But if he is made of flesh and is like the rest, he will not be able to accomplish this, but on the contrary if he reestablishes what is missing, he might rule alone. This is why some people fail to notice this occurring when it does.

(*Anonymus Iamblichi* fr. 6 and 7 = DK 89, 6; Vol. 2 402.21–404.32)

Suggestions for Further Reading

All of these entries have further bibliographies. Complete bibliographical information for collections may be found in the bibliography in the Introduction, pp. 10–12. See also the relevant chapters in Barnes; Guthrie; McKirahan; and Kirk, Raven, and Schofield.

Adkins, A. W. H. 1960. *Merit and Responsibility: A Study in Greek Values.* Oxford: Clarendon Press.

Balot, R. K. 2001. *Greed and Injustice in Classical Athens.* Princeton: Princeton University Press.

Barney, R. "The Sophistic Movement," in Gill and Pellegrin, pp. 77–97.

Bett, R. 2002. "Is There a Sophistic Ethics?" *Ancient Philosophy* 22: pp. 235–62.

———. 1989. "The Sophists and Relativism." *Phronesis* 34: pp. 169–89.

Cole, A. T. 1961. "The Anonymous Iamblichi and His Place in Greek Philosophical Thought." *Harvard Studies in Classical Philology* 65: pp. 127–63.

De Romilly, J. 1992. *The Great Sophists in Periclean Athens,* translated by J. Lloyd. Oxford: Clarendon Press, Oxford University Press.

Dover, K. 1974. *Greek Popular Morality in the Time of Plato and Aristotle.* Oxford: Basil Blackwell.

Gagarin, M., and P. Woodruff, eds. 1995. *Early Greek Political Thought from Homer to the Sophists.* Cambridge: Cambridge University Press.

———. "The Sophists." in Curd and Graham, pp. 365–82.

Kahn, C. 1981. "The Origins of Social Contract Theory in the Fifth Century B.C.," in Kerferd 1981b, pp. 92–108.

Kerferd, G. B. 1981a. *The Sophistic Movement.* Cambridge: Cambridge University Press.

———, ed. 1981b. *The Sophists and Their Legacy.* Wiesbaden: Steiner.

———. 1997. "The Sophists," in Taylor, pp. 244–70.

Osborne, R. "The Polis and Its Culture," in Taylor, pp. 9–46.

Pendrick, G., ed. and trans. 2002. *Antiphon the Sophist: The Fragments.* Cambridge: Cambridge University Press.

Robinson, T. M. 1979. *Contrasting Arguments: An Edition of the "Dissoi Logoi."* New York: Arno Press.

Sprague, R. K., ed. 1972, rep. 2001. *The Older Sophists.* Indianapolis: Hackett.

15. THE DERVENI PAPYRUS, COLUMNS IV–XXVI

The Derveni Papyrus was found in 1962, by workers constructing a highway in northern Greece, near the town of Derveni. It is a scroll, partially burnt and otherwise damaged (it was used in a funeral pyre in about 400 BCE), which contains parts of an Orphic poem with a commentary on the poem. Orpheus was a mythological musician and son of Apollo, who went to Hades and returned. Orphism is based on this myth, and the central texts of Orphism were based on material that supposedly went back to Orpheus himself. A fundamental belief was that the soul is immortal and undergoes transmigrations from one body to another. Following the Orphic way of life, after undergoing initiation, was supposed to bring eventual freedom from transmigration and release from punishment after death. The Derveni Papyrus combines an Orphic theogony similar to Hesiod's, along with a naturalizing explanation of the Orphic poem.[1] The author, who is familiar with Presocratic theories, interprets the theogony as an allegorical cosmology, and in doing so quotes Heraclitus and offers explanations that seem to indicate familiarity with Anaxagoras and perhaps Diogenes of Apollonia.

The papyrus contains twenty-six columns of text, all of which are more or less damaged; the first three columns contain practically no legible material, so our text begins with column IV.[2] The author weaves together quotations of parts of the Orphic poem with his commentary.

1. In the Orphic poem, there is first Night, who gives birth to Ouranos [the heavens]. Ouranos rules but is overthrown by Kronos, who is, in turn, overthrown by Zeus. It is Zeus who is responsible for the present state of the cosmos.

2. McKirahan describes it this way: "Imagine a rolled up newspaper partially burned in a fire, whose outer pages are destroyed, as are the top and bottom of the remaining pages, in which the fire, heat, and subsequent handling have created holes of varying sizes" (*Philosophy Before Socrates*, 2nd edition, p. 430).

Note on the text: McKirahan uses the conventions of three dots and square brackets to indicate gaps in the text. Three dots indicate a gap that he does not attempt to fill. Square brackets indicate supplements that seem likely. Question marks indicate supplements that are less certain. Angle brackets enclose material that is not in the Greek and is added for reasons of style. Parentheses are used for Greek words and English synonyms.

Column IV

. . . In the same way, Heraclitus [? using as evidence] things that are common, [overturns] things that are private, saying like an [? astronomer], "the sun . . . by its nature is the width of a human foot, not exceeding [? in size the limits of its width. Otherwise] the Erinyes, [the ministers of Justice] will find him out. . . .

Column V

. . . for them we enter the oracular shrine to [? inquire], for the sake of those who are seeking oracles, whether it is right. . . . Why do they disbelieve in the terrors of Hades? Since they do not understand dreams or any of the other things, what examples would be the grounds for their belief? [? For] overcome by error and pleasure as well they [neither] learn [nor] believe. Disbelief and failure to understand [? are the same thing. For if] they [neither] learn nor understand [it is not possible that they will believe] even when they see. . . .

Column VI

. . . prayers and sacrifices propitiate the [souls], and [the incantation] of the magi is able to remove the divinities that are in the way; divinities that are in the way [? are the enemies of souls]. For this reason the magi [perform] the sacrifice as if they are paying a penalty. On the offerings they pour water and milk, and from these they also make libations to the dead. They offer countless round knobby cakes because the souls too are countless. Initiates make a preliminary sacrifice to the Eumenides in the same way as the magi do, for the Eumenides are souls. On account of these things anyone who is going to sacrifice to the gods first [? must sacrifice] a bird. . . .

Column VII

. . . a hymn saying sound and lawful things. For [. . .] in the poem, and it is not possible to say [. . .] of words and the things that have been spoken. The poem is [alien] and enigmatic for people. [Orpheus] himself did not want to utter riddles that may be contested, but great matters in riddles. In fact he is narrating a holy discourse from the first word to the last, as [he shows] in the easily understood [verse]. For after bidding them to "put doors on their ears," he says that [he is not legislating for the] many . . . those [pure] in hearing . . .

Column VIII

. . . he shows [in this] verse:

who were born from Zeus, the [exceedingly mighty] king.
And how they begin he shows in this:
When Zeus from his father took the prophesied rule
and the strength in his hands, and the glorious divinity.

It is not noticed that these words are transposed. This is how they should be taken: "When Zeus took the strength from his father and the glorious divinity." When taken this way . . . not that Zeus hears [his father] but that he takes the strength [from him]. If taken [the other way he might seem to have taken the strength] contrary to the prophecies. . . .

Column IX

. . . So he made the [strength] belong to the most powerful just as a son belongs to his father. But those who do not understand what is said think that Zeus takes both the strength and the divinity from his own father. Now knowing that when fire is mixed up with the other things it agitates the things that are and prevents them from combining because of fomentation, he removed it far enough for it not, once it is removed, to prevent the things that are from being compounded. For whatever is kindled is dominated, and when dominated it is mixed with the other things. But regarding the words "he took in his hands," he was speaking in riddles as he was with the other things [? that previously appeared unclear, but which have been understood] with complete certainty. [Speaking in riddles,] then, he said that Zeus [took] by force [the strength and the] divinity just as if . . .

Column X

. . . and speaking; for it is [not] possible to speak without uttering. But he thought that speaking and uttering are the same. Also speaking and teaching mean the same thing. For it is impossible to teach without speaking whatever is taught through speech. Also, teaching is thought to take place through speaking. Therefore teaching was not considered separate from speaking, nor speaking from uttering, but uttering, speaking and teaching [mean] the same. Thus [nothing prevents] "all-uttering" and "teaching all things" from being the same thing. By calling her "nurse" he says in riddles that whatever the sun dissolves [by heating] the night [combines by cooling]. . . whatever the sun heated.

Column XI

. . . of Night. [He says] that she "proclaims oracles from the [innermost shrine (*aduton*)]," intending that the depth of the night is "never setting" (*aduton*). [For] it does not set as the light does, but the sunlight overtakes it as it remains in the same place. Further, "proclaim oracles" and "assist" mean the same thing. But it is important to consider what "assist" and "proclaim oracles" apply to. "Believing that this god proclaims oracles, they come to find out what they should do." [After this] he says:

[And she] proclaimed all that it was [right] for him [to accomplish] . . .

Column XII

. . . The next verse goes as follows:

In order that he might [? rule] on the lovely dwelling place of snow-clad Olympus.

Olympus and time are the same thing. Those who think that Olympus and the heaven are the same are completely mistaken. They do not understand that the heaven cannot be longer rather than wider, but if someone were to call time long he would not be completely mistaken.

Whenever he wanted to say "heaven" he added the epithet "wide," while whenever <he wanted to say> ["Olympus"] he never <added> "wide," [but "long"]. By saying that it is "snow-clad" he virtually [? likens time to what is] snowy; what is snowy [? is cold and] white . . .

Column XIII

When Zeus, having heard the prophecies from his father.

For he did not hear this, but it has been shown in what way he heard. Nor does Night give orders, but he makes it clear by saying as follows:

He swallowed the genital organ, who was first to spring out of the Aithēr.

Because in all his poetry he is speaking in riddles about things, it is necessary to discuss each word individually. Seeing that people believe that generation depends on the [genital organs] and that without the genital organs there is [no] coming to be, he used this <word>, likening the sun to a genital organ, since without the sun it would be impossible for the things that are to come to be as they are. . . .

Column XIV

. . . spring out of the brightest and hottest, which had been separated from himself. So he says that this Kronos was born to Helios (Sun) and Gē (Earth), because it was through the sun that he <Kronos> was the cause of their <the things that are> striking against one another. This is why he says, "who did a great deed."

And the next verse,

Ouranos (Heaven), son of Evening, who was the first of all to reign.

Mind that strikes (krouonta) <the things that are> against one another he named Kronos and says that he did a great deed to Ouranos, since he deprived him of the kingship. He named him Kronos from his deed and <he named> the other things according to the [same] principle. For when all the things that are [? were not yet being struck, Mind,] as [? defining (horizōn)] nature, [? received the designation Ouranos. He

says that he] was deprived [of his kingship] when the things that are [?
were being struck].

Column XV

. . . [? in order to prevent the heat from] striking them <the things that
are> against one another, and [in order to] make the things that are
separate for the first time and stand apart from one another. For when
the sun was being separated and confined in the middle, <Mind> coag-
ulated them and it holds them fast, both those above the sun and those
below. And the next verse:

After him in turn <reigned> Kronos, and then Zeus wise in
counsel.

He means something like "from that time is the beginning from which
the present rule reigns." It is related [that Mind,] by striking the things
that are against one another and setting them apart toward their present reconfiguration, [did] not [make] them become different things, but
things with different [qualities]. The words "and then [Zeus wise in
counsel" make it clear] that it <Mind> is not different but the same. And
he indicates this: "counsel . . . royal honor."

Column XVI

It has been shown [that] he called the sun a [genital organ]. He also says
that the things that are now come to be from things that exist:

Of the genital organ of the first born king, on which all
the immortals grew, blessed gods and goddesses,
and rivers and lovely springs, and all other things
that had then been born, and he himself, therefore, came to be
alone.
[He is now] king of all things [and will be] in the future.

In these verses he indicates that the things that are existed always and
the things that are now come to be from things that exist. As for <the
phrase>, "he himself, therefore, came to be alone," in saying this he
shows that Mind, being alone, is worth everything [as] if the others were
nothing. For without Mind it is not possible for the things that are now

to be [? through them]. [Further in the next verse after this he said that Mind] is worth everything:

[? Clearly] Mind and [? the king of all things are the] same thing.

Column XVII

It existed before it was named. Then it was named. For air was a thing that is before the things that are now were formed, and it always will be. For it did not come to be, but it was. Why it was called air has been shown above. It was thought to have come to be because it had been named Zeus, as if it previously were not a thing that is. And he said that this will be "last" because it was named Zeus, and this will continue to be its name until the things that are now are formed into the same state in which they were previously floating as things that are. He [shows] that it is because of this <namely, air> that the things that are came to be such, and, having come to be, [? again] in this. . . . He indicates in the following words:

Zeus is the head, [Zeus the middle], and from Zeus all things [? are fashioned].

Head . . . he speaks in riddles . . . head . . . comes to be the beginning of formation . . . is formed . . .

Column XVIII

. . . and the things moving downward . . . saying . . . that this [earth] and all other things are in the air, being breath. Now Orpheus named this breath Moira [Fate]. Other people commonly say "Moira has spun for them" and "all that Moira has spun will be," speaking correctly but not knowing what either Moira or spinning is. For Orpheus called intelligence Moira, for this appeared to him the most suitable of the names that all people had given, since before it was called Zeus there existed Moira, the intelligence of the god, always and everywhere. But when it had been called Zeus, [it was thought] that he had come to be, even though he existed before without being named. [This is why he says] "Zeus came to be first." . . .

Column XIX

. . . the things that are are called each one after what dominates. According to the same principle all things were called Zeus. For air dominates all things as much as it wishes. In saying "Moira spun" they are saying that the intelligence of Zeus sanctioned the way in which the things that are, the things that come to be, and the things that will be should come to be and be and cease. He likens the air to a king—for among the names that are spoken this appeared to be appropriate to it—saying as follows:

Zeus the king, Zeus the ruler of all, he of the bright thunderbolt.

He says that he is [king] because one [of the authorities <namely, the royal authority>] has power over [? all the others] . . . and accomplishes all things. . . .

Column XX

. . . of people in cities, after performing the sacred rites, they saw. I wonder less that they do not understand. For it is impossible to hear what is being said and to learn it at the same time. But people who <have heard the rites> from a person who makes the holy rites his craft deserve to be wondered at and pitied: wondered at because before they performed the rites they think they will gain knowledge, but after performing them they go away before gaining knowledge, without even asking further questions, as if they had gained knowledge of the things they saw or heard or learned; and pitied because it was not enough that they spent their money in advance, but they go away deprived of their judgment as well. Before performing the rites they hoped that they would gain knowledge, but after performing them they go away deprived even of their hope. . . .

Column XXI

. . . nor the cold to the cold. By saying "jump" he shows that divided up into small pieces, they were moving and jumping in air, and as they were jumping the pieces of each kind were set together with one another. They continued to jump until each of them came to its like. Aphrodite Ourania (Heavenly Aphrodite) and Zeus, "aphrodizing" and jumping,

Peithō (Persuasion) and *Harmonia* ("joining") are established as names of the same god. A man mingling with a woman is commonly said to aphrodize. Since the things that are now were mingled with one another, <the god> was named Aphrodite, and <he was named> *Peithō* because the things that are yielded to one another; yielding and persuading are the same thing. <He was named> *Harmonia* because he joined many of the things that are to each of them. For they existed previously [too], but were named as coming to be after they were separated apart. . . .

Column XXII

. . . [so] he named all things similarly, in the best way he could, knowing the nature of men, that they do not all have a like <nature> or want the same things. When they have power, each of them says whatever may come to his heart, whatever they may happen to want, never the same things, out of greed, and some things out of ignorance too. Gē (Earth), Mētēr (Mother), Rhea, and Hera are the same; she was called Gē by custom, Mētēr because all things come to be from her, Gē and Gaia according to each person's dialect. She was named Demeter as in Gē Mētēr—a single name from both, because they are the same. It is also said in the Hymns, "Demeter Rhea Gē Mētēr Hestia Dēiō." For she is called Dēiō because she was ravaged (*edēiōthē*) in the mingling. He will make it clear [. . .] in the verses that she [? is born]. <She is called> Rhea because many and . . . animals grew . . . from her.

Column XXIII

This verse is composed in a way that makes it misleading, and it is unclear to the many, although for those who understand correctly it is very clear that Oceanos is air and air is Zeus. Therefore it was not another Zeus that "contrived" Zeus, but Zeus himself contrived for himself "great strength." But those who do not understand suppose that Oceanos is a river because he added the epithet "wide-flowing." But he indicates his own meaning in customary words that are in current use. For people say that those who have great power "have flowed big." The next <verse>,

He inserted the sinews of silver-eddying Achelous.

[gives] the name Achelous to water. . . .

Column XXIV

. . . are equal measured from the middle, but those that are not circular cannot be equal-limbed. This makes it clear:

which shines for many mortals over the boundless earth.

Someone might suppose that this verse was said in a different sense, namely that if <the moon> is full, the things that are appear more than before it was full. But he does not mean that it is shining, for if this is what he meant he would have said not that it shines "for many" but "for all" at once—both those who work the land and those who sail when it is time for them that they should sail. For if there were no moon, people would not have discovered how to reckon the seasons or the winds . . . and everything else. . . .

Column XXV

. . . and brightness. But those of which the moon <is composed> are the whitest of all, divided according to the same principle, but they are not hot. There are others too now in air floating far from one another, but by day they are invisible because they are dominated by the sun, while at night it is evident that they are. They are dominated on account of their smallness. Each of them floats in necessity in order for them not to come together with one another. Otherwise all that have the same property as those from which the sun was formed would come together in a mass. If the god did not want the things that are now to exist, he would not have made the sun. But he made it the sort and size of thing as is related at the beginning of the account. The following <words> he composes as a blind, [not] wanting everyone to understand. He indicates in the following verse:

[but when the mind] of Zeus [contrived all] deeds.

Column XXVI

. . . "of mother" because Mind is the mother of the other things. "Good" because she is good. He makes it clear in the following verses as well that he means good.

Hermes, son of Maia, messenger, giver of good things.

He also makes it clear in the following:

At Zeus's threshold are placed two jars
of gifts such as they give—one of evils, one of goods.

Those who do not understand the word suppose it is "of his own mother." But if he wanted to show the god "wanting to mingle in love of his own mother," by altering the letters he could have said "of his mother," for in that way it would become "of his own," and he would be her [son].

Suggestions for Further Reading

All of these entries have further bibliographies. Complete bibliographical information for collections may be found in the bibliography in the Introduction, pp. 10–12. See also the relevant chapters in McKirahan; and Kirk, Raven, and Schofield.

Betegh, G. 2004. *The Derveni Papyrus: Cosmology, Theology, and Interpretation.* Cambridge: Cambridge University Press.

Kouremenos, T., G. M. Parássoglou, and K. Tsantsanoglou. 2006. *The Derveni Papyrus.* Firenze: L. S. Olschki.

Laks, A., and G. W. Most. 1997. *Studies on the Derveni Papyrus.* Oxford: Oxford University Press.

Parker, R. 1995. "Early Orphism." In *The Greek World,* edited by A. Powell, pp. 483–510. London and New York: Routledge.

CONCORDANCE

Democritus (DK68)	10. Atomism
A1	55
A37	5
A38	6
A40	39
A47	10, 22, 23, 26
A48b	14
A57	32
A58	20, 25
A59	9
A60	27
A66	28, 29
A68	30
A93	41
A104	42
A112	50
A129	35
A135	36, 43
B6	47
B7	49
B8	48
B9	44, 46
B11	45
B33	59
B69	57
B74	56
B117	51
B125	52
B155	33
B156	16
B164	38
B166	53
B189	60
B191	54
B214	58
B235	61

Diogenes of Apollonia (DK64)	13. Diogenes of Apollonia
A1	9
A6	10
A19	11
B1	1
B2	2

B36	102
B38	70
B42	73
B44	75
B43	72
B45	76
B46	77
B47	74
B48	78
B53	71
B54	71
B55	80
B56	81
B57	103
B58	104
B59	107
B60	105
B61	106
B62	95
B64	96
B65	98
B66	97
B67	99
B68	100
B71	82
B73	84
B75	91
B76	50
B78	6
B79	93
B80	94
B81	61
B82	89
B83	92
B84	109
B85	85
B86	86
B87	109
B88	108
B90	69
B91	56
B92	59
B93	60

B94	79
B96	87
B98	88
B99	110
B100	111
B101	112
B102	113
B104	114
B105	119
B106	117
B107	118
B108	120
B109	115
B110	116
B111	31
B112	1
B113	3
B114	2
B115	8
B117	12
B118	14
B119	13
B121	15
B124	16
B125	10
B126	11
B127	25
B128	4
B129	3; Pythagoras 5
B130	5
B131	29
B132	7
B133	28
B134	66
B135	21
B136	17
B137	19
B138	18
B139	53
B140	23
B141	24
B142	9
B144	22

B76	51
B78	42
B80	57
B82	70
B83	76
B84a	55
B85	109
B86	9
B87	31
B88	82
B89	20
B90	49
B91	40
B92	113
B93	16
B94	88
B95	108
B96	99
B97	32
B98	65
B99	90
B101	37
B101a	63
B102	77
B103	79
B104	8
B107	13
B108	10
B110	107
B111	84
B112	18
B113	17
B114	23
B115	44
B116	35
B117	54
B118	53
B119	106
B120	91
B121	100
B123	12
B124	78
B125	56

Parmenides (DK28)   **6. Parmenides**

B1	1
B2	2
B3	3
B4	4
B5	5
B6	6
B7	7
B8	8
B9	9
B10	10
B11	11
B12	12
B13	13
B14	14
B15	15
B16	16
B17	17
B18	18
B19	19

Pherecydes (DK36)

B4	Pythagoras 4

Philolaus (DK44)   **12. Philolaus**

B1	1
B2	2
B3	3
B4	4
B5	5
B6	6
B6a	7
B7	8
B8	13
B13	12
B16	10
B17	9
B20	11

Prodicus (DK84)   **14. Sophists**

B5	17

A32	30
A33	34
A38	32
A39	35
A40	31
A44	33
B1	1
B2	2
B7	3; Pythagoreans 1
B8	4
B10	5
B11	6
B12	7
B14	8
B15	9
B16	10
B17	11
B18	Introduction, p. 5; 12
B23	13
B24	14
B25	16
B26	15
B27	17
B28	18
B29	19
B30	20
B31	21
B32	22
B33	23
B34	24
B35	25
B36	26
B38	27

Zeno (DK 29)	**7. Zeno**
A11	1
A12	1
A16	2
B1	4
B2	3
B3	5
A24	12
A25	6, 8